GET RESULTS!

World Facts

D1485915

GET RESULTS!

World Facts

GEDDES & GROSSET

Published by Geddes & Grosset,
David Dale House, New Lanark ML11 9DJ, Scotland

First published 1998
Reprinted 1999, 2001 (twice), 2003 (twice), 2005, 2007

© 1998 Geddes & Grosset

Cover photograph by Dale O'Dell, courtesy of the Stock Market

ISBN 978 1 85534 384 9

Printed and bound in India

Countries of the World

Afghanistan

A landlocked country in southern Asia. The greater part of the country is mountainous with a central mass of huge mountain ranges. The climate is generally arid with great extremes of temperature and considerable snowfall in winter. The country experiences many earthquakes and periods of severe drought. The main economic activity is agriculture although only 15 per cent of the land is suitable for farming. Its main exports have been Karakul lambskins, raw cotton, fruit and nuts, and opium. Afghanistan has suffered from ongoing war and conflict during its modern history to the extent that its economy and infrastructure have been severely affected. After the Russian withdrawal from Afghanistan in 1989, the country was troubled by mainly ethnic conflict. In 1996, the Taleban, a fundamentalist Islamic group, took control of the country. In 2001, they in turn were forced to withdraw from most of Afghanistan by a united US, Allied and Northern Alliance force. By 2005, the country was being governed by a democratically elected president and national assembly although fighting has continued in a small area of the country still controlled by Taleban forces.

Quick facts:

Area: 251,773 square miles (652,225 square kilometres)

Population: 20,833,000

Capital: Kabul

Other cities: Herat, Kandahar, Mazar-i-Sharif

Form of government: Islamic Republic

Religions: Sunni Islam, Shia Islam

Currency: Afghani

Albania

A small mountainous country in the Balkan region of south-eastern Europe. Its immediate neighbours are GREECE, Serbia and Montenegro and the Former Yugoslav Republic of MACEDONIA and it is bounded to the west by the Adriatic Sea. The climate is typically Mediterranean and although most rain falls in winter, severe thunderstorms frequently occur on the plains in summer. Winters are severe in the highland areas and heavy snowfalls are common. All land is state-owned, with the main agricultural areas lying along the Adriatic coast and in the Korce Basin and about a fifth of the land being arable. Industry is also nationalised and output is small. The principal industries are agricultural product processing, textiles, oil products, cement, iron and steel. Albania has been afflicted by severe economic problems and in late 1996 public dissatisfaction with the government erupted into civil unrest, leading to a major revolt by citizen militias during which the government forces lost control. By March 1997 the country was on the brink of collapse and large numbers of refugees were leaving. The situation was reversed, however, when ethnic cleansing of Albanian inhabitants of the Kosovo region of Serbia in 1999 led to a flood of refugees into Albania (and elsewhere). NATO bombing ended the cleansing and Kosovar Albanians were able to return home.

Quick facts:

Area: 11,009 square miles (28,748 square kilometres)

Population: 3,581,000

Capital: Tirana (Tiranè)

Other cities: Durrès, Shkodèr, Vlorë

Form of government: Socialist Republic

Religion: Sunni Islam, Albanian Orthodox, Roman Catholicism

Currency: Lek

Algeria

A huge country in northern Africa that fringes the Mediterranean Sea in the north. Over four-fifths of Algeria is covered by the Sahara Desert to the south. Near the north coastal area the Atlas Mountains run east-west in parallel ranges. The Chelif, at 450 miles (724 kilometres) long, is the country's main river, rising in the Tell Atlas and flowing to the Mediterranean. The climate in the coastal areas is warm and temperate with most of the rain falling in winter. The summers are dry and hot with temperatures rising to over 89°F (32°C). Inland beyond the Atlas Mountains conditions become more arid and temperatures range from 120°F (49°C) during the day to 50°F (10°C) at night. Most of Algeria is unproductive agriculturally, but it does possess one of the largest reserves of natural gas and oil in the world. Algeria's main exports are oil-based products, fruit, vegetables, tobacco, phosphates and cork, while imports include textiles, foodstuffs, machinery, iron and steel. In recent years, the country has been racked by civil strife and terrorist attacks, with the various opposing forces unable to agree peace proposals.

Quick facts:
Area: 919,595 square miles (2,381,741 square kilometres)
Population: 29,168,000
Capital: Algiers (Alger, El Djazair)
Other cities: Oran, Constantine, 'Annaba
Form of government: Republic
Religion: Sunni Islam
Currency: Algerian Dinar

American Samoa see SAMOA, AMERICAN.

Andorra

A tiny state, situated high in the eastern Pyrénées, between FRANCE and SPAIN. The state consists of deep valleys and high mountain peaks which reach heights of 9,843 feet (3,000 metres). Although only 12 miles (20 kilometres) wide and 19 miles (30 kilometres) long, the spectacular scenery and climate attract many tourists. About 10 million visitors arrive each year, during the cold weather when heavy snowfalls make for ideal skiing, or in summer when the weather is mild and sunny and the mountains are used for walking. Tourism and the duty-free trade are now Andorra's chief sources of income. Natives who are not involved in the tourist industry may raise sheep and cattle on the high pastures. Although Andorra has no airport or railroad, there is a good road system. The average life expectancy from birth is 95 for women, 86 for men and 91 years overall. In 1993 an Andorran government was elected and has its own Parliament after 715 years of being ruled by France's leader and the Spanish Bishop of Urgel.

Quick facts:
Area: 175 square miles (453 square
  kilometres)
Population: 65,900
Capital: Andorra la Vella
Form of government: Republic
Religion: Roman Catholicism
Currency: Euro

Angola

Situated on the Atlantic coast of southern Africa, Angola lies about 10°S of the equator. It shares borders with CONGO, DEMOCRATIC REPUBLIC OF CONGO, ZAMBIA and NAMIBIA. Its climate is tropical with temperatures constantly between 68°F (20°C) and 77°F (25°C). The rainfall is heaviest in inland areas where there are vast equatorial forests. The country is also rich in minerals, however deposits of manganese, copper and phosphate are as yet unexploited. Diamonds are mined in the northeast and oil is produced near Luanda. Oil production is the most important aspect of the economy, making up about 90 per cent of exports which have traditionally included diamonds, fish, coffee and palm oil. Around 70 per cent of the workforce are engaged in agriculture. Since independence from Portugal in 1975, the United States is the main recipient of the country's exports. However, the Angolan economy has been severely damaged by the civil war of the 1980s and early 1990s.

Quick facts:

Area: 481,354 square miles (1,246,700 square kilometres)

Population: 11,185,000

Capital: Luanda

Other cities: Huambo, Lobito, Benguela, Lubango

Form of government: People's Republic

Religions: Roman Catholicism, traditional beliefs

Currency: Kwanza

Anguilla

An island in the Leeward Islands group of the Caribbean Sea, now a self-governing British dependency. From 1967 until 1980 it was in federation with ST CHRISTOPHER (ST KITTS) AND NEVIS. The country's main source of revenue is tourism and lobsters account for half of the island's exports.

Quick facts:

Area: 37 square miles (96 square kilometres)

Population: 12,400

Capital: The Valley

Form of government: British Overseas Territory

Religion: Christianity

Currency: East Caribbean Dollar

Antigua and Barbuda

Located on the eastern side of the Leeward Islands, Antigua and Barbuda is a tiny state comprising three islands – Antigua, Barbuda and the uninhabited rocky islet of Redonda. Antigua's strategic position was recognised by the British in the 18th century when it was an important naval base and later by the USA who built the island's airport during World War II to defend the Caribbean and the Panama Canal. Although mainly low-lying, the country's highest point is Boggy Peak at 1,329 feet (405 metres). The climate is tropical although its average rainfall of 4 inches (100 millimetres) makes it drier than most of the other islands of the West Indies. Tourism is the main industry as its numerous sandy beaches make it an ideal destination. Barbuda is surrounded by coral reefs and the island is home to a wide range of wildlife. Cotton, sugar cane and fruits are cultivated and fishing is an important industry in Barbuda. Great damage was inflicted on Antigua and Barbuda in 1995 by Hurricane Luis when over 75 per cent of property was destroyed or damaged.

Quick facts:

Area: 171 square miles (442 square kilometres)
Population: 66,000
Capital: St John's
Form of government: Constitutional Monarchy
Religion: Christianity (mainly Anglicanism)
Currency: East Caribbean Dollar

Argentina

The world's eighth largest country, which stretches from the Tropic of Capricorn to Cape Horn on the southern tip of the South American continent. To the west a massive mountain chain, the Andes, forms the border with CHILE. The climate ranges from warm temperate over the Pampas in the central region, to a more arid climate in the north and west, while in the extreme south conditions although also dry are much cooler. The vast fertile plains of the Pampas are the main agricultural area and produce cereals and wheat, while in other irrigated areas sugar cane, fruit and grapes for wine are raised. Meat processing, animal products and livestock production are major industries and also feature prominently in export trade. A series of military regimes and ongoing political and economic crises have resulted in an unstable economy which fails to provide reasonable living standards for the population.

Quick facts:
Area: 1,073,518 square miles (2,780,400 square kilometres)
Population: 39,920,000
Capital: Buenos Aires
Other cities: Cordoba, Rosario, Mar del Plata, Mendoza, La Plata, Salta
Form of government: Federal Republic
Religion: Roman Catholicism
Currency: Peso

Armenia

The smallest republic of the former USSR and part of the former kingdom of Armenia, which was divided between TURKEY, IRAN and the former USSR. It declared independence from the USSR in 1991. It is a landlocked Transcaucasian republic and its neighbours are TURKEY, IRAN, GEORGIA and AZERBAIJAN. The country is very mountainous, with many peaks over 9,900 feet (3,000 metres), the highest being Arragats Lerr at 13,435 feet (4,095 metres). Agriculture is mixed in the lowland areas. The main crops grown are grain, sugar beet and potatoes, and livestock reared include cattle, pigs and sheep. Mining of copper, zinc and lead is important, and to a lesser extent gold, aluminium and molybdenum, and industrial development is increasing. Hydroelectricity is produced from stations on the River Razdan as it falls 3,281 feet (1,000 metres) from Lake Sevan to its confluence with the River Araks. Territorial conflict with Azerbaijan over Nagorny Karabakh under a ceasefire since 1994 put a brake on economic development for many years.

Quick facts:

Area: 11,506 square miles (29,800 square kilometres)
Population: 2,796,000
Capital: Yerevan
Other major city: Kunmayr (Gyumri)
Form of government: Republic
Religion: Armenian Orthodox
Currency: Dram

Aruba

A Caribbean island off the coast of Venezuela, until 1986 one of the NETHERLANDS ANTILLES. It is a self-governing dependency of the Netherlands. The development of tourism began here in the 1980s.

Quick facts:

Area: 75 square miles (193 square kilometres)

Population: 87,000

Capital: Oranjestad

Form of government: Self-governing Dutch Territory

Religion: Christianity

Currency: Aruban Florin

Australia

The world's smallest continental landmass is a vast and sparsely populated island state in the southern hemisphere and is comprised of seven states. The most mountainous region is the Great Dividing Range, which runs down the entire east coast. Because of its great size, Australia's climates range from tropical monsoon to cool temperate and also large areas of desert. The majority of the country's natural inland lakes are salt water and are the remnants of a huge inland sea. The Great Barrier Reef is approximately 1,250 miles (2,000 kilometres) long and is the largest coral formation known in the world. Central and south Queensland are subtropical while north and central New South Wales are warm temperate. Much of Australia's wealth comes from agriculture, with huge sheep and cattle stations extending over large parts of the interior known as the Outback. Australia is the world's leading producer of wool, particularly the fine merino wool. Cereal growing is dominated by wheat. Mining continues to be an important industry and produces coal, natural gas, oil, gold and iron ore. Australia is the largest producer of diamonds.

Quick facts:

Area: 2,988,902 square miles (7,741,220 square kilometres)

Population: 20,264,000

Capital: Canberra

Other cities: Adelaide, Brisbane, Melbourne, Perth, Sydney

Form of government: Federal Parliamentary State

Religion: Christianity

Currency: Australian Dollar

Austria

A landlocked country in central Europe surrounded by seven nations. The wall of mountains that runs across the centre of the country dominates the scenery. In the warm summers tourists come to walk in the forests and mountains and in the cold winters skiers come to the mountains that now boast over 50 ski resorts. The main river is the Danube and there are numerous lakes, principally Lake Constance (Bodensee) and Lake Neusiedler. Agriculture is based on small farms, many of which are run by single families. Dairy products, beef and lamb from the hill farms contribute to exports. More than 37 per cent of Austria is covered in forest, resulting in the paper-making industry near Graz. There are mineral resources of lignite, magnesium, petroleum, iron ore and natural gas and high-grade graphite is exported. Unemployment is very low and its low strike record has attracted multinational companies in recent years. Attachment to local customs is still strong and in rural areas men still wear lederhosen and women the traditional dirndl skirt on feast days and special occasions.

Quick facts:
Area: 32,378 square miles (83,859 square
  kilometres)
Population: 8,192,000
Capital: Vienna (Wien)
Other cities: Graz, Linz, Salzburg, Innsbruck
Form of government: Federal Republic
Religion: Roman Catholicism
Currency: Euro

Azerbaijan

A republic of the former USSR that declared itself independent in 1991. It is situated on the southwest coast of the Caspian Sea and shares borders with IRAN, ARMENIA, GEORGIA and RUSSIA. The Araks river separates Azerbaijan from the region known as Azerbaijan in northern Iran. The country is semi-arid and 70 per cent of the land is irrigated for the production of cotton, wheat, maize, potatoes, tobacco, tea and citrus fruits. It has rich mineral deposits of oil, natural gas, iron and aluminium. The most important mineral is oil, which is found in the Baku area from where it is piped to Batumi on the Black Sea. There are steel, synthetic rubber and aluminium works at Sumqayit just north of the capital, Baku. However, Azerbaijan is only minimally developed industrially and is hindered by its dispute with Armenia over the Nagorny-Karabakh region.

Quick facts:

Area: 33,436 square miles (86,600 square kilometres)
Population: 7,961,000
Capital: Baku
Other major city: Sumqayit
Form of government: Republic
Religions: Shia Islam, Sunni Islam, Russian Orthodox
Currency: Manat

Bahamas, The

The Bahamas consist of an archipelago of 700 islands located in the Atlantic Ocean off the southeast coast of Florida. The largest island is Andros (1,600 square miles/4,144 square kilometres) and the two most populated are Grand Bahama and New Providence where the capital, Nassau, lies. Winters in the Bahamas are mild and summers warm. Most rain falls in May, June, September and October and thunderstorms are frequent in summer. The islands are also subject to hurricanes and other tropical storms. The islands have few natural resources and for many years fishing and small-scale farming (citrus fruits and vegetables) were the only ways to make a living. Now, however, tourism, which employs almost half the workforce, is the most important industry and has been developed on a vast scale. Offshore banking is also a growing source of income. About three million tourists, mainly from North America, visit the Bahamas each year.

Quick facts:
Area: 5,358 square miles (13,878 square
   kilometres)
Population: 284,000
Capital: Nassau
Other major city: Freeport
Form of government: Constitutional Monarchy
Religion: Christianity
Currency: Bahamian Dollar

Bahrain

A Gulf State comprising 33 low-lying islands situated between the QATAR peninsula and the mainland of SAUDI ARABIA. Bahrain Island is the largest, and a causeway, called the King Fahd Causeway, linking it to Saudi Arabia was opened in 1986. The highest point in the state is only 402 feet (122 metres) above sea level. The climate is pleasantly warm between December and March, but very hot from June to November. Most of Bahrain is sandy and too saline to support crops but drainage schemes are now used to reduce salinity and fertile soil is imported from other islands. Oil was discovered in 1931 and revenues from oil now account for about 80 per cent of the country's total revenue. Bahrain is being developed as a major manufacturing state, the main enterprises being aluminium smelting and the manufacture of clothing, paper products and consumer goods. Traditional industries include pearl fishing, boat building, weaving and pottery. Agricultural products include vegetables, dates and fruits, with artesian wells providing irrigation mainly on the north coast.

Quick facts:

Area: 268 square miles (694 square kilometres)
Population: 698,000
Capital: Manama (Al Manamah)
Form of government: Hereditary Monarchy
Religions: Shia Islam, Sunni Islam
Currency: Bahraini Dinar

Bangladesh

Formerly the eastern province of PAKISTAN, Bangladesh is the world's eighth most populated country. It is bounded almost entirely by INDIA and to the south by the Bay of Bengal. There is a wide variety of animal life, with the Sundarbans area being one of the last strongholds of the Bengal tiger. The country is extremely flat and is virtually a huge delta formed by the Ganges, Brahmaputra AND Meghna rivers. The country is subject to devastating floods and cyclones that sweep in from the Bay of Bengal. Most villages are built on mud platforms to keep them above water. The climate is tropical monsoon with heat, extreme humidity and heavy rainfall in the monsoon season (April to October) along with accompanying tornadoes. The short winter season is mild and dry. The combination of rainfall, sun and silt from the rivers makes the land productive and it is often possible to grow three crops a year. Bangladesh produces about 70 per cent of the world's jute and the production of jute-related products is a principal industry, with tea being an important cash crop. There are few mineral resources although natural gas, coal and peat are found.

Quick facts:
Area: 55,598 square miles (143,998 square
   kilometres)
Population: 147,365,000
Capital: Dhaka
Other cities: Chittagong, Khulna, Narayanganj,
   Saidpur
Form of government: Republic
Religions: Sunni Islam, Hinduism
Currency: Taka

Barbados

The most easterly island of the West Indies, lying well outside the group of islands that make up the Lesser Antilles. Mainly surrounded by coral reefs, most of the island is low-lying and only in the north does it rise to 1,104 feet (336 metres) at Mount Hillaby. The climate is tropical, but the cooling effect of the northeast trade winds prevents the temperatures rising above 86°F (30°C). There are only two seasons, the dry and the wet, when rainfall is very heavy. At one time the economy depended almost exclusively on the production of sugar and its by-products, molasses and rum and although the industry is now declining, sugar is still the principal export. Tourism has now taken over as the main industry, employing approximately 40 per cent of the island's labour force, although there are industries manufacturing furniture, clothing, electrical and electronic equipment. More recently, deposits of natural gas and petroleum have been discovered and fishing is an important activity. The island is surrounded by pink and white sandy beaches and coral reefs that are visited by around 400,000 tourists each year.

Quick facts:
Area: 166 square miles (430 square kilometres)
Population: 279,000
Capital: Bridgetown
Form of government: Parliamentary Democracy
Religions: Anglicanism, Methodism
Currency: Barbados Dollar

Belarus (Belorussia, Byelorussia)
A republic of the former USSR that declared itself independent in 1991. It borders POLAND to the west, UKRAINE to the south, LATVIA and LITHUANIA to the north, and RUSSIA to the east. The country consists mainly of a low-lying plain, and forests cover approximately one-third of the land. The climate is continental, with long severe winters and short warm summers. Although the economy is overwhelmingly based on industry, including oil refining, food processing, woodworking, chemicals, textiles and machinery, output has gradually declined since 1991 and problems persist in the supply of raw materials from other republics that previously were part of the USSR. Agriculture, although seriously affected by contamination from the Chernobyl nuclear accident of 1986, accounts for approximately 20 per cent of employment, the main crops being flax, potatoes and hemp. The main livestock raised are cattle and pigs. Extensive forest areas also contribute in the supply of raw materials for woodwork and paper-making. Peat is the fuel used to provide power for industry and the country's power plants. Belarus has a good transport system of road, rail, navigable rivers and canals.

Quick facts:
Area: 80,155 square miles (207,600 square kilometres)
Population: 10,293,000
Capital: Minsk
Other cities: Homyel (Gomel), Vitsyebsk, Mahilyov
Form of government: Republic
Religions: Russian Orthodox, Roman Catholicism, Islam
Currency: Belarusian Ruble

Belau see PALAU.

Belgium

A highly industrialised, relatively small country in northwest Europe with a short coastline on the North Sea. The Meuse river divides Belgium into two distinct geographical regions. To the north of the river the land slopes continuously for 93 miles (150 kilometres) until it reaches the North Sea where the coastlands are flat and grassy. To the south of the river is the forested plateau area of the Ardennes. Between these two regions lies the Meuse valley. Belgium is a densely populated country with few natural resources. Agriculture, which uses about 45 per cent of the land for cultivation or rearing of livestock, employs only 3 per cent of the workforce. About one-fifth of the country is covered with forests, with the wooded areas mainly used for recreation. The metal-working industry, originally based on the small mineral deposits in the Ardennes, is the most important industry, and in the northern cities new textile industries are producing carpets and clothing. Nearly all raw materials are now imported through the main port of Antwerp. There are three officially recognised languages in Belgium – Flemish (Dutch), French and German.

Quick facts:

Area: 11,783 square miles (30,519 square kilometres)

Population: 10,379,000

Capital: Brussels

Other cities: Antwerp, Charleroi, Ghent, Liège, Oostende

Form of government: Constitutional Monarchy

Religion: Roman Catholicism

Currency: Euro

Belize

A small Central American country on the southeast of the Yucatan Peninsula in the Caribbean Sea. Its coastline on the Gulf of Honduras is approached through some 550 kilometres (342 miles) of coral reefs and keys (cayo). The coastal area and north of the country are low-lying and swampy with dense forests inland. In the south the Maya Mountains rise to 1100 metres (3609 feet). The subtropical climate is warm and humid and the trade winds bring cooling sea breezes. Rainfall is heavy, particularly in the south and hurricanes may occur in summer. The dense forests that cover most of the country provide valuable hardwoods such as mahogany. Most of the population make a living from forestry, fishing, or agriculture, although only 5 per cent of the land is cultivated. The main crops grown for export are sugar cane, citrus fruits (mainly grapefruit), bananas and coconuts. Industry is very underdeveloped, causing many people to emigrate to find work. The official language is English although many others are spoken, including Mayan, Carib and Spanish.

Quick facts:
Area: 8,763 square miles (22,696 square
    kilometres)
Population: 287,000
Capital: Belmopan
Other major city: Belize City
Form of government: Parliamentary Democracy
Religions: Roman Catholicism, Protestantism
Currency: Belizean Dollar

Belorussia see Belarus.

Benin

An ice cream cone-shaped country with a very short coastline on the Bight of Benin on the southern coast of West Africa. The coastal area has white sandy beaches backed by lagoons and low-lying fertile lands known as barre country. In the northwest the Atakora Mountains are grassy plateaus that are deeply cut into steep forested valleys and on the grasslands sheep, cattle and goats are reared. The main rivers of Benin are the Donga, Couffo and Niger with its tributaries. The climate in the north is tropical and in the south equatorial. There are nine rainy months each year so crops rarely fail. Farming is predominantly subsistence and accounts for around 60 per cent of employment, with yams, cassava, maize, rice, groundnuts and vegetables forming most of the produce. The country is very poor, although since the late 1980s economic reforms have been towards a market economy and Western financial aid has been sought. The main exports are palm oil, palm kernels and cotton. Tourism is now being developed but as yet facilities for this are few except in some coastal towns.

Quick facts:

Area: 43,484 square miles (112,622 square kilometres)
Population: 7,862,000
Capital: Porto-Novo
Other major city: Cotonou
Form of government: Republic
Religions: Traditional beliefs, Roman Catholicism, Sunni Islam
Currency: CFA Franc

Bermuda

A country consisting of a group of 150 small islands in the western Atlantic Ocean. It lies about 572 miles (920 kilometres) east of Cape Hatteras on the coast of the United States. The hilly limestone islands are the caps of ancient volcanoes rising from the sea bed. The main island, Great Bermuda, is linked to the other islands by bridges and causeways. The climate is warm and humid, with rain spread evenly throughout the year but with the risk of hurricanes from June to November. Bermuda's chief agricultural products are fresh vegetables, bananas and citrus fruit, but 80 per cent of food requirements are imported. Many foreign banks and financial institutions operate from the island, taking advantage of the lenient tax laws. Other industries include ship repair and pharmaceuticals. Its proximity to the USA and the pleasant climate have led to a flourishing tourist industry.

Quick facts:
Area: 20 square miles (53 square kilometres)
Population: 64,000
Capital: Hamilton
Form of government: British Overseas Territory
Religions: Protestantism, Roman Catholicism
Currency: Bermudan Dollar

Bhutan

A country that is surrounded by INDIA to the south and CHINA to the north. It rises from foothills overlooking the Brahmaputra river to the southern slopes of the Himalayas. The Himalayas, which rise to over 24,600 feet (7,500 metres) in Bhutan, make up most of the country. The climate is hot and wet on the plains but temperatures drop progressively with altitude, resulting in glaciers and permanent snow cover in the north. The valleys in the centre of the country are wide and fertile, and about 95 per cent of the workforce are farmers growing wheat, rice, potatoes and corn. Fruit such as plums, pears, apples and also cardamom are grown for export. There are many monasteries, with about 6,000 monks. Yaks reared on the high pasture land provide milk, cheese and meat. Vast areas of the country still remain forested as there is little demand for new farmland. Bhutan is one of the world's poorest and least developed countries. It has little contact with the rest of the world although tourism has been encouraged in recent years. There are no railways but roads join many parts of the country.

Quick facts:
Area: 18,147 square miles (47,000 square
    kilometres)
Population: 2,279,000
Capital: Thimphu
Form of government: Constitutional Monarchy
Religions: Buddhism, Hinduism
Currency: Ngultrum

Bolivia

A landlocked republic of central South America through which the great mountain range of the Andes runs. It is in the Andes that the highest navigable lake in the world, Lake Titicaca, is found. On the undulating depression south of the lake, the Altiplano, is the highest capital city in the world, La Paz. To the east and northeast of the mountains is a huge area of lowland containing tropical rainforests (the Llanos) and wooded savanna (the Chaco). The northeast has a heavy rainfall while in the southwest it is negligible. Temperatures vary with altitude, from extremely cold on the summits to cool on the Altiplano, where at least half the population lives. Although rich in natural resources such as lead, silver, copper, zinc, oil and tin, Bolivia remains a poor country because of lack of funds for their extraction, lack of investment and political instability. Bolivia is self-sufficient in petroleum and exports natural gas. Agriculture produces soya beans, sugar cane and cotton for export, and increased production of coca, from which cocaine is derived, has resulted in an illicit economy.

Quick facts:
Area: 424,165 square miles (1,098,581 square
  kilometres)
Population: 8,989,000
Capital: La Paz (administrative), Sucre (legal)
Other cities: Cochabamba, Santa Cruz, Oruro,
  Potosi
Form of government: Republic
Religion: Roman Catholicism
Currency: Boliviano

Bosnia-Herzegovina

A republic of former Yugoslavia that was formally recognised as an independent state in March 1992. It is a very mountainous country and includes part of the Dinaric Alps, which are densely forested and deeply cut by rivers flowing northwards to join the Sava river. Half the country is forested, and lumber is an important product of the northern areas. One quarter of the land is cultivated, and corn, wheat and flax are the principal products of the north. In the south, tobacco, cotton, fruits and grapes are the main products. Bosnia-Herzegovina has large deposits of lignite, iron ore and bauxite, and its metallurgical plants create air pollution. Water is also polluted around these, with a shortage of drinking water, the Sava river being severely affected. Despite the natural resources the economy has been devastated by civil war, which began in 1991 following the secession of CROATIA and SLOVENIA from the former Yugoslavia. Dispute over control of Bosnia-Herzegovina continued, leading to United Nations intervention in an attempt to devise a territorial plan acceptable to all factions. A peace agreement signed in late 1995 has resulted in the division of the country into two self-governing provinces. The population of the state was significantly diminished when refugees from the civil war fled between 1992 and 1993.

Quick facts:

Area: 19,735 square miles (51,129 square kilometres)
Population: 4,510,000
Capital: Sarajevo
Other cities: Banja Luka, Mostar, Tuzla
Form of government: Republic
Religions: Eastern Orthodox, Sunni Islam, Roman Catholicism
Currency: Marka

Botswana

A landlocked republic in southern Africa that straddles the Tropic of Capricorn. Much of the west and southwest of the country forms part of the Kalahari Desert. In the north there is a huge area of marshland around the Okavango Delta, which is home for a wide variety of wildlife. With the exception of the desert area, most of the country has a subtropical climate but is subject to drought. In winter, days are warm and nights cold while summer is hot with sporadic rainfall. The people are mainly farmers and cattle rearing is the main activity. After independence in 1966, the exploitation of minerals started. In 1972 the first diamond mine was set up at Orapa, and diamonds quickly became the country's most important export, and copper from the nickel/copper complex at Selebi-Pikwe was also exported. Exploitation of these mineral resources has facilitated a high rate of economic growth within the country. Coal is also mined but the majority is for domestic use. About 17 per cent of the land is set aside for wildlife preservation in national parks, game reserves, game sanctuaries and controlled hunting areas.

Quick facts:

Area: 224,607 square miles (581,730 square kilometres)
Population: 1,639,000
Capital: Gaborone
Other cities: Francistown, Molepolole, Mahalapye
Form of government: Republic
Religions: Traditional beliefs, Christianity
Currency: Pula

Brazil

A huge South American country bounded to the north, south and east by the Atlantic ocean. It is the fifth largest country in the world and covers nearly half of South America. The climate is mainly tropical, but altitude, distance from the sea and prevailing winds cause many variations. The Amazon river basin occupies a huge area of land, over one-third of the country's area, and much of this is covered by tropical rainforests. In the tropical areas winters are dry and summers wet and droughts may occur in the northeast where it is hot and arid. About 14 per cent of the population is employed in agriculture, which occupies only about 7 per cent of the land area, and the main products exported are coffee, soya beans, orange juice and cocoa. Brazil is rich in minerals and is the only source of high grade quartz crystal in commercial quantities. It is also a major producer of chrome ore, and it is now developing what is thought to be the richest iron ore deposits in the world. Since improvement of facilities, fishing is now an important industry, mainly of lobsters, shrimp and sardines.

Quick facts:
Area: 3,300,171 square miles (8,547,403 square kilometres)
Population: 188,078,000
Capital: Brasília
Other cities: Balem, Belo Horizonte, Curitiba, Porto Alegre, Recife, Rio de Janeiro, Salvador, São Paulo
Form of government: Federal Republic
Religion: Roman Catholicism
Currency: Real

Brunei

A sultanate located on the northwest coast of the island of Borneo in Southeast Asia. It is bounded on all sides by the Sarawak territory of MALAYSIA, which splits the sultanate into two separate parts. Broad tidal swamplands cover the coastal plains, and inland Brunei is hilly and covered with tropical rainforests that occupy almost half the country's land area. The climate is tropical marine, hot and moist, with cool nights. Rainfall is heavy (98 inches/2,500 millimetres) at the coast but even heavier (197 inches/5,000 millimetres) inland. The main crops grown are rice, vegetables and fruit, but economically the country depends on its oil industry, which employs 7 per cent of the working population. Cloth weaving and metalwork are also small local industries. Oil production began in the 1920s and now oil and natural gas account for almost all exports. Other minor products are rubber, pepper, gravel and animal hides.

Quick facts:
Area: 2,226 square miles (5,765 square kilometres)
Population: 379,000
Capital: Bandar Seri Begawan
Other cities: Kuala Belait, Seria
Form of government: Monarchy (Sultanate)
Religion: Sunni Islam
Currency: Bruneian Dollar

Bulgaria

A southeast European republic located on the east Balkan peninsula and with a coast on the Black Sea. It is bounded to the north by ROMANIA, to the west by Serbia and Montenegro and the Former Yugoslav Republic of MACEDONIA, and to the south by GREECE and TURKEY. The centre of Bulgaria is crossed from west to east by the Balkan Mountains. The south of the country has a Mediterranean climate with hot dry summers and mild winters. Farther north the temperatures become more extreme and rainfall is higher in summer. The main river in Bulgaria is the Danube, and about a third of the country is covered by forests. Traditionally Bulgaria is an agricultural country and a revolution in farming during the 1950s led to great increases in output. This was because of the collectivisation of farms and the use of more machinery, fertilisers and irrigation. Increased mechanisation led to more of the workforce being available to work in mines and industry. However, the country suffered very high rates of inflation and unemployment in the early 1990s after the break-up of the former Soviet Union and it has struggled to achieve a transition to democracy and a market economy. Living standards remain low. Despite concerns about corruption and organised crime, Bulgaria became a member of the European Union at the beginning of 2007.

Quick facts:
Area: 42,823 square miles (110,912 square
   kilometres)
Population: 7,385,000
Capital: Sofiya (Sofia)
Other cities: Burgas, Plovdiv, Ruse, Varna
Form of government: Republic
Religion: Eastern Orthodox
Currency: Lev

Burkina Faso (Burkina)

A landlocked state in West Africa, Burkina (formerly called Upper Volta) lies on the fringe of the Sahara, to the north. It comprises a plateau region in the north which gives way southwards to an area of plains. The northern part of the country is arid and is more or less an extension of the Sahara Desert. The south is less dry and has savanna-type vegetation and scattered trees. Precipitation is generally low, the heaviest rain falling in the southwest, while the rest of the country is semi-desert. The dusty grey plains in the north and west have infertile soils that have been further impoverished by overgrazing and over-cultivation. About 85 per cent of the people live by subsistence farming and food crops include sorghum, millet, pulses, corn and rice. The main industries are textiles, metal products and the processing of agricultural products and production of consumer items such as footwear and soap. Cotton is the main export, along with minerals such as gold and animal products. There is great poverty and shortage of work and many of the younger population go to GHANA and CÔTE D'IVOIRE for employment. During the 1970s the country was severely affected by drought and this was followed by political instability in the 1980s. The situation has improved since the 1990s.

Quick facts:
Area: 105,792 square miles (274,000 square
  kilometres)
Population: 13,902,000
Capital: Ouagadougou
Other cities: Bobo-Dioulasso, Koudougou
Form of government: Republic
Religions: Traditional beliefs, Sunni Islam
Currency: CFA Franc

Burma see MYANMAR.

Burundi

A small, densely populated country in central east Africa, bounded by RWANDA to the north, TANZANIA to the east and south and the Democratic Republic of CONGO to the west. One of the poorest nations in the world, Burundi consists mainly of an upland plateau at an elevation of 4,600–5,900 feet (1,400–1,800 metres). The climate is equatorial but modified by altitude. The savanna in the east is several degrees hotter than the plateau and there are two wet seasons. The soils are not rich but there is enough rain to grow crops in most areas for subsistence farming. The main food crops are bananas, sweet potatoes, peas, lentils and beans. Cassava is grown near the shores of Lake Tanganyika which is in the Great Rift Valley. The main cash crop is coffee, which accounts for 90 per cent of Burundi's export earnings. Cotton and tea are also cultivated for export. There is a little commercial fishing on Lake Tanganyika, otherwise industry is very basic. Since 1994 Burundi has been afflicted by ethnic conflict between the majority Hutu and minority Tutsi. Between 1994 and 1995 it is estimated that 150,000 were killed as a result of ethnic violence and the political situation remains highly volatile.

Quick facts:
Area: 10,747 square miles (27,834 square
   kilometres)
Population: 8,090,000
Capital: Bujumbura
Form of government: Republic
Religion: Roman Catholicism, traditional beliefs
Currency: Burundi Franc

Byelorussia see BELARUS.

Cambodia

A southeast Asian state bounded by THAILAND, LAOS and VIETNAM, with its southern coast lying on the Gulf of Thailand. The country was devastated by its involvement in the Vietnam War (1960–75) followed by the brutal regime of the Khymer Rouge under Pol Pot (1975–79). The heart of the country is saucer-shaped, and gently rolling alluvial plains are drained by the Mekong river. The Dangrek Mountains form the frontier with Thailand in the north-west. In general Cambodia has a tropical monsoon climate and about half the land is tropical forest. During the rainy season the Mekong swells and backs into the Tônlé Sap (Great Lake), increasing its size threefold to about 4,015 square miles (10,400 kilometres). This seasonal flooding means the area is left with rich silt when the river recedes. Crop production depends entirely on the rainfall and floods but production was badly disrupted during the civil war when there was widespread famine, and yields still remain low. The cultivation of rice accounts for about 80 per cent of agricultural land and the other main crop is rubber, which grows in the eastern plateau. Despite the gradual rebuilding of the infrastructure in the early 1990s, Cambodia remains one of the world's poorest nations.

Quick facts:
Area: 69,898 square miles (181,035 square kilometres)
Population: 13,881,000
Capital: Phnom-Penh
Other cities: Battambang, Kampong Cham
Form of government: People's Republic
Religion: Buddhism
Currency: Riel

Cameroon

A triangular-shaped country of diverse landscapes in west central Africa. It stretches from Lake Chad at its apex to the northern borders of EQUATORIAL GUINEA, GABON and the CONGO in the south. The landscape ranges from low-lying lands, through the semi-desert Sahel to dramatic mountain peaks and then to the grassy savanna, rolling uplands, steaming tropical forests and hardwood plantations. Cameroon's jungles contain not only commercially valuable trees but also an immense diversity of other plants, many of which have been identified as useful for their medicinal properties. Farther south are the volcanoes, including the sporadically active Mount Cameroon, the highest peak at 1,250 feet (4,100 metres) and the palm beaches at Kribi and Limbe. The climate is equatorial with high temperatures and plentiful rain. The majority of the population are farmers who live in the south and in central Cameroon where they grow maize, millet, cassava and vegetables. In the drier north, where drought and hunger are well known, life is harder and this area is populated by semi-nomadic herders. Bananas, coffee and cocoa are the major exports although oil, gas and aluminium are becoming increasingly important.

Quick facts:
Area: 183,569 square miles (475,442 square
  kilometres)
Population: 17,340,000
Capital: Yaoundé
Other major city: Douala
Form of government: Republic
Religions: Traditional beliefs, Roman
  Catholicism, Sunni Islam
Currency: CFA Franc

Canada

The second largest country in the world and the largest in North America. Canada is a land of great climatic and geographical extremes. It lies to the north of the UNITED STATES and has Pacific, Atlantic and Arctic coasts. The country has the highest number of inland waters and lakes in the world, including the Great Lakes on the border with the USA. The Rocky Mountains and Coast Mountains run down the west side and the highest point, Mount Logan (19,524 feet/6,050 metres), is in the Yukon. Climates range from polar conditions in the north to cool temperate in the south, with considerable differences from west to east. More than 80 per cent of its farmland is in the prairies that stretch from Alberta to Manitoba. Wheat and grain crops cover three-quarters of the arable land. Canada is rich in forest reserves, which cover more than half the total land area. The most valuable mineral deposits (oil, gas, coal and iron ore) are found in Alberta. Most industry in Canada is associated with processing its natural resources and it is one of the main exporters of food products.

Quick facts:
Area: 3,849,674 square miles (9,970,610 square kilometres)
Population: 33,098,000
Capital: Ottawa
Other cities: Calgary, Toronto, Montréal, Vancouver, Québec City, Winnipeg
Form of government: Federal Parliamentary State
Religions: Roman Catholicism, United Church of Canada, Anglicanism
Currency: Canadian Dollar

Cape Verde

One of the world's smallest nations, situated in the Atlantic Ocean about 400 miles (640 kilometres) northwest of SENEGAL. It consists of ten islands and five islets and there is an active volcano on Fogo, one of the islands. The islands are divided into the Windward group and the Leeward group. Over 50 per cent of the population live on São Tiago on which is Praia, the capital. The climate is arid with a cool dry season from December to June and warm dry conditions for the rest of the year. Rainfall is sparse and the islands suffer from periods of severe drought. Agriculture is mostly confined to irrigated inland valleys and the chief crops are coconuts, sugar cane, potatoes, cassava and dates. Bananas and some coffee are grown for export. Fishing for tuna and lobsters is an important industry but in general the economy is shaky and Cape Verde relies heavily on foreign aid. Because of its lack of natural resources and droughts, large numbers of its people have emigrated for many years. Tourism is being encouraged although the number of visitors is at present relatively low.

Quick facts:

Area: 1,557 square miles (4,033 square kilometres)
Population: 420,000
Capital: Praia
Form of government: Republic
Religion: Roman Catholicism
Currency: Cape Verdean Escudo

Cayman Islands

A group of three low-lying coral islands in the Caribbean Sea, 149 miles (240 kilometres) south of Cuba. They are a British Overseas Territory. The group comprises Grand Cayman, by far the largest of the three, Cayman Brac and Little Cayman (the name is derived from the Carib Indian word for 'crocodile'). The Cayman Islands are a popular destination for cruise liners, and a tax haven.

Quick facts:
Area: 102 square miles (264 square kilometres)
Population: 45,000
Capital: George Town, on Grand Cayman
Form of government: British Overseas Territory
Religion: Christianity
Currency: Cayman Islands Dollar

Central African Republic

A landlocked country in central Africa bordered by CHAD in the north, CAMEROON in the west, SUDAN in the east and the CONGO and Democratic Republic of CONGO in the south. The terrain consists of 2,000–3,000 feet (610–915 metres) high undulating plateaus with dense tropical forest in the south and a semi-desert area in the east. The climate is tropical with little variation in temperature throughout the year. The wet months are May, June, October and November. Floods and tornadoes can occur at the beginning of the rainy season. Most of the population live in the west and in the hot, humid south and southwest. Over 86 per cent of the working population are subsistence farmers and the main crops grown are cassava, groundnuts, bananas, plantains, millet and maize. Livestock rearing is small-scale because of the prevalence of the tsetse fly. Gems and industrial diamonds are mined and deposits of uranium, iron ore, lime, zinc and gold have been discovered, although they remain relatively undeveloped. The country's main exports are coffee, diamonds, cotton, tobacco and lumber, although this is hampered by the distance from a port. Since the country's independence in 1960, its political and economic fortunes have been mixed.

Quick facts:
Area: 240,535 square miles (622,984 square
    kilometres)
Population: 4,303,000
Capital: Bangui
Other cities: Bambari, Bangassou
Form of government: Republic
Religions: Traditional beliefs, Roman
    Catholicism
Currency: CFA Franc

Chad

A landlocked country in the centre of northern Africa that extends from the edge of the equatorial forests in the south to the middle of the Sahara Desert in the north. It lies more than 944 miles (1,600 kilometres) from the nearest coast. The climate is tropical, with adequate rainfall in the south, but the north experiences semi-desert conditions. In the far north of the country the Tibesti Mountains rise from the desert sand more than 11,200 feet (3,415 metres). The southern part of Chad is the most densely populated and its relatively well-watered savanna has always been the country's most arable region. Unless there is drought, this area is farmed for cotton (the main cash crop along with livestock exports), millet, sorghum, groundnuts, rice and vegetables. Fishing is carried out in the rivers and in Lake Chad. Cotton ginning and manufacture of peanut oil are the principal industries. As a result of drought and civil war, Chad has become one of the poorest countries in the world. In 2003 it became an oil-producing country but a lack of infrastructure, ongoing unrest within the country and conflict with neighbouring Sudan mean that poverty is still rife and the economy continues to suffer.

Quick facts:

Area: 495,755 square miles (1,284,000 square
   kilometres)
Population: 9,944,000
Capital: N'Djamena
Other cities: Sarh, Moundou, Abéché
Form of government: Republic
Religions: Sunni Islam, traditional beliefs
Currency: CFA Franc

Chile

A country that lies like a backbone down the Pacific coast of the South American continent with the Andes Mountains extending its length. Its Pacific coastline is 2,600 miles (4,184 kilometres) long and the country is liable to volcanic explosions and earthquakes. Because of its enormous range in latitude it has almost every kind of climate, from desert conditions to icy wastes. The north, in which lies the Atacama Desert, is extremely arid. The Atacama Desert is rich in mineral deposits and has large quantities of nitrates. The climate of the central region is Mediterranean and that of the south cool temperate. Sixty per cent of the population live in the central valley where the climate is similar to that of southern California. The land here is fertile and the principal crops grown are grapes, wheat, apples, sugar beet, maize, tomatoes and potatoes. There is also a significant wine-making industry. It is also in the central valley that the vast copper mine of El Teniente is located. This is one of the largest copper mines in the world and accounts for Chile's most important source of foreign exchange.

Quick facts:
Area: 292,135 square miles (756,626 square kilometres)
Population: 16,134,000
Capital: Santiago
Other cities: Arica, Concepcion, Valparaiso, Viña del Mar
Form of government: Republic
Religion: Roman Catholicism
Currency: Chilean Peso

China

The third largest country in the world, China covers a large area of East Asia and also includes over 3,400 islands. In western China most of the terrain is very inhospitable. In the northwest there are deserts that extend into MONGOLIA and RUSSIA, and much of the southwest consists of the ice-capped peaks of TIBET. The southeast has a green and well-watered landscape comprising terraced hillsides and paddy fields. Its main rivers are the Yangtze, Huang He and Xi Jiang. Most of China has a temperate climate but in such a large country wide ranges of latitude and altitudes produce local variations. Intensive cultivation and horticulture are necessary to feed its population of over one billion. After the death of Mao Tse-tung in 1976 and under the leadership of Deng Xiaoping, China experienced huge modernisation in agriculture and industry as a result of the supply of expertise, capital and technology from Japan and the West. The country was opened up to tourists and, to a degree, adopted the philosophy of free enterprise, resulting in a dramatic improvement in living standards for a significant proportion of the population. The change towards a market economy, however, created some internal political problems. Pro-democracy demonstrations in 1989 resulted in the Tianmen Square massacre, raising questions regarding China's approach to human rights.

Quick facts:

Area: 3,705,408 square miles (9,596,961 square kilometres)
Population: 1,313,973,000
Capital: Beijing (Peking)
Other cities: Chengdu, Guangzhou, Harbin, Shanghai, Tianjin, Wuhan
Form of government: People's Republic
Religions: Buddhism, Confucianism, Taoism
Currency: Yuan

Colombia

A country situated in the north of South America, most of it lying between the equator and 10 degrees north. The Andes, which split into three ranges (the Cordilleras) in Colombia, run north along the west coast and gradually disappear towards the Caribbean Sea. Half of Colombia lies east of the Andes and much of this region is covered in tropical grassland. Towards the Amazon Basin the vegetation changes to tropical forest. The climates in Colombia include equatorial and tropical, according to altitude. Very little of the country is under cultivation although much of the soil is fertile. The range of climates results in an extraordinary variety of crops, of which coffee is the most important and includes cocoa beans, sugar cane, bananas, cotton and tobacco. Colombia is rich in minerals such as gold, silver, platinum and copper and produces about half of the world's emeralds. It is South America's leading producer of coal, and petroleum is the country's most important foreign revenue earner. However, Colombia has also experienced violence and conflict, involving not only guerrilla groups but also the country's sizable illegal drug trade.

Quick facts:

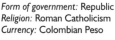

Area: 439,737 square miles (1,138,914 square kilometres)
Population: 43,593,000
Capital: Bogotá
Other cities: Barranquilla, Cali, Cartagena, Medellin
Form of government: Republic
Religion: Roman Catholicism
Currency: Colombian Peso

Comoros, The

A country that consists of three volcanic islands in the Indian Ocean, situated between mainland Africa and MADAGASCAR. Physically, four islands make up the group but the island of Mayotte remained a French dependency when the three western islands became a federal Islamic republic in 1975. The islands are mostly forested and the tropical climate is affected by Indian monsoon winds from the north. There is a wet season from November to April that is accompanied by cyclones. Only small areas of the islands are cultivated and most of this land belongs to foreign plantation owners. The chief product was formerly sugar cane but now vanilla, copra, maize, cloves and essential oils are the most important products. The forests provide lumber for building and there is a small fishing industry. The coelacanth (a primitive bony fish), previously thought to have been extinct for millions of years, was discovered living in the seas off the Comoros in 1938.

Quick facts:
Area: 720 square miles (1,865 square kilometres) excluding Mayotte
Population: 690,000
Capital: Moroni
Other cities: Dornoni, Fomboni, Mutsamudu, Mitsamiouli
Form of government: Islamic Republic
Religion: Sunni Islam
Currency: Comoran Franc

El Salvador

The smallest and most densely populated state in Central America. It is bounded north and east by HONDURAS and has a Pacific coast to the south. Two volcanic ranges run from east to west across the country and the country is also susceptible to earthquakes. The Lempa river cuts the southern ranges in the centre of the country and opens as a large sandy delta to the Pacific Ocean. Although fairly near the equator, the climate tends to be warm rather than hot and the highlands have a cooler temperate climate. The country is predominantly agricultural and 32 per cent of the land is used for crops such as coffee (the major crop and revenue earner), cotton, maize, beans, rice and sorghum, and a slightly smaller area is used for grazing cattle, pigs, sheep and goats. Fishing is carried out, the most important being shrimp, although tuna, mackerel and swordfish are also caught. A few industries such as food processing, textiles and chemicals are found in the major towns. The country suffers from a high rate of inflation and unemployment and is one of the poorest countries in the Americas as a result of civil war in the 1980s and natural disasters such as Hurricane Mitch in 1998.

Quick facts:

Area: 8,124 square miles (21,041 square kilometres)
Population: 6,8226,000
Capital: San Salvador
Other cities: Santa Ana, San Miguel
Form of government: Republic
Religion: Roman Catholicism
Currency: Colon/US Dollar

Equatorial Guinea

A country that lies about 124 miles (200 kilometres) north of the equator on the hot humid coast of west Africa. The country consists of a square-shaped mainland area (Mbini), with its few small offshore islets, and the islands of Bioko and Pagalu (Anno-bon). The climate is tropical and the wet season in Bioko and Pegalu lasts from December to February. Bioko is a very fertile volcanic island, and it is here that the capital, Malabo, is situated beside a volcanic crater flooded by the sea. It is also the centre of the country's cocoa production. Coffee and lumber are produced for export on the mainland. Large gas and oil deposits were discovered in the 1990s and the country is now one of sub-Saharan Africa's biggest oil producers with a fast-growing economy. However, the benefits of these oil revenues have not yet reached the country's people under the brutal rule of their president, Obiang Nguema.

Quick facts:
Area: 10,830 square miles (28,051 square kilometres)
Population: 540,000
Capital: Malabo
Other major city: Bata
Form of government: Republic
Religion: Roman Catholicism
Currency: CFA Franc

Eritrea

Formerly an autonomous province of ETHIOPIA that gained independence in May 1993, shortly after a landslide vote in favor of sovereignty. Bounded by DJIBOUTI, SUDAN and ETHIOPIA, Eritrea acquired Ethiopia's entire coastline along the Red Sea. The small Eritrean port of Aseb, in the southeast corner of the country, was designated a 'free port' guaranteeing the right of access for the now landlocked Ethiopia but there have been many border disputes around this and other issues since then. Eritrea's climate is hot and dry along its desert coast but is colder and wetter in its central highland regions. Most of the population depend on subsistence farming. Future revenues may come from developing fishing, tourism and oil industries. Eritrea's natural resources include gold, potash, zinc, copper, salt, fish and probably oil. Deforestation and the consequent erosion are partly responsible for the frequent droughts and resultant famines that have blighted this area in recent years. Many of the population have been displaced by famine or in the border conflict with Ethiopia but a fragile peace is now in place as the country tries to rebuild its economy.

Quick facts:
Area: 45,406 square miles (117,600 square
    kilometres)
Population: 4,786,000
Capital: Asmara (Asmera)
Other cities: Mits'iwa, Keren, Assab (Aseb)
Form of government: Republic
Religions: Sunni Islam, Christianity
Currency: Nakfa

Estonia

A country that has over 1,500 islands and lies to the northwest of Russia and is bounded to the north by the Gulf of Finland, to the west by the Baltic Sea and to the south by Latvia. It is the smallest of the three previous Soviet Baltic Republics. Agriculture and dairy farming are the chief occupations and there are nearly three hundred agricultural collectives and state farms. The main products are grain, potatoes, flax, vegetables, meat, milk and eggs. Livestock includes cattle, sheep, goats and pigs. Almost 22 per cent of Estonia is forested, mainly with aspen, pine, birch and fir, and this provides material for sawmills, furniture, match and pulp industries. The country has rich, high quality shale deposits and phosphorous has been found near Tallinn. Peat deposits are substantial and supply some of the electric power stations. Estonia has about 72 per cent of its population living in urban areas, with almost a third living in the capital city. The economy has undergone a major transformation to a free market system. Tourism and investment from the West have greatly contributed to the country's economy and it became a member of the European Union in 2004.

Quick facts:
Area: 17,413 square miles (45,227 square kilometres)
Population: 1,324,000
Capital: Tallinn
Other cities: Tartu, Narva, Pärnu
Form of government: Republic
Religions: Eastern Orthodox, Lutheranism
Currency: Estonian Kroon

Ethiopia

A landlocked, East African country with borders with SUDAN, KENYA, SOMALIA, DJIBOUTI and ERITREA. Most of the country consists of highlands that drop sharply toward SUDAN in the west. Because of the wide range of latitudes, Ethiopia has many climatic variations between the high temperate plateau and the hot humid lowlands. The country is very vulnerable to drought but in some areas thunderstorms can erode soil from the slopes, reducing the area available for crop planting. Around 80 per cent of the population are subsistence farmers, and there are mineral deposits of copper, iron, petroleum, platinum and gold, which have been exploited. Coffee is the main source of rural income and teff is the main food grain. The droughts in 1989–90 brought much famine. Employment outside agriculture is confined to a small manufacturing sector in Addis Ababa. The country has been racked with environmental, economic and political problems and by its long-lasting border war with ERITREA.

Quick facts:

Area: 426,373 square miles (1,104,300 square
　kilometres)
Population: 58,506,000
Capital: Addis Ababa (Adis Abeba)
Other cities: Dire Dawa, Gonder, Jima
Form of government: Federal Republic
Religions: Ethiopian Orthodox, Sunni Islam
Currency: Ethiopian Birr

Faeroe (Faroe) Islands (Føroyar)

A self-governing part of DENMARK since 1948. They consist of a group of 18 basaltic islands and are situated in the North Atlantic, approximately halfway between the Shetland Islands and Iceland. The landscape of these islands is characterised by steep, stepped peaks rising out of the sea to nearly 3,000 feet (900 metres) and glaciated, trough-shaped valleys. Although the islands are inhabited, poor agricultural conditions compel the population to seek their living at sea. Fishing, including some whaling, is the main occupation and exports comprise fish and associated products.

Quick facts:
Area: 540 square miles (1,399 square kilometres)
Population: 47,000
Capital: Tórshavn
Form of government: Self-governing region of Denmark
Religion: Lutheranism
Currency: Danish Krone

Falkland Islands

A British Overseas Territory situated in the South Atlantic, consisting of two large islands (West and East Falkland), separated by the 10-mile (16-kilometre) wide Falkland Sound and surrounded by some 200 smaller islands. Lying about 410 miles (650 kilometres) east of southern Argentina, these islands were invaded by Argentina in 1982. Argentina had long laid claim to these 'Islas Malvinas' but they were recaptured by a British marine task force a few months later. The main economic activity is sheep farming, with open grazing on the wind-swept, treeless, rugged moorland that rises to over 2,295 feet (705 metres) on both main islands. The highest point is Mount Usborne at 2,313 feet (705 metres). Over recent years, substantial income has been gained from the sales of licences to permit foreign trawlers to fish in the Falklands exclusion zone. There are also considerable offshore oil reserves available.

Quick facts:
Area: 4,700 square miles (12,173 square
   kilometres)
Population: 2,967
Capital: Stanley
Form of government: British Overseas Territory
Religion: Christianity
Currency: Falkland Pound

Fiji

One of the largest nations in the western Pacific, consisting of some 800 islands and atolls of which only about 100 are inhabited. It is situated around the 180-degree International Date Line and lies about 17 degrees south of the equator. Fiji has high rainfall, high temperatures and plenty of sunshine all year round. The two main islands, Viti Levu and Vanua Levu, are extinct volcanoes, and most of the islands in the group are fringed with coral reefs. The southeast of the islands have tropical rainforests but a lot of lumber has been felled and soil erosion is a growing problem. The main cash crop is sugar cane although copra, ginger and fish are also exported. In 1993, Cyclone Kina caused great destruction to agriculture and the general infrastructure. Tourism has been a major industry and source of revenue but it has been adversely affected by ongoing political coups and racial unrest.

Quick facts:
Area: 7,056 square miles (18,274 square kilometres)
Population: 905,000
Capital: Suva
Form of government: Republic
Religions: Christianity, Hinduism
Currency: Fijian Dollar

Finland

A Scandinavian country that shares borders with SWEDEN, NORWAY and RUSSIA. Its coastline lies along the Gulf of Bothnia and the Gulf of Finland, both of which are arms of the Baltic Sea. Some 30,000 islands and islets line Finland's coast. Finnish Lapland in the north lies within the Arctic Circle. Most of mainland Finland is low-lying, becoming more hilly towards the north. Almost three-quarters of the country is forested, comprising mainly coniferous trees such as spruce and pine, and there are many thousands of lakes. The climate has great extremes between summer and winter. Winter is very severe and lasts about six months but only for three months in the south. Summers are short but quite warm, with light rain throughout the country. Finland is largely self-sufficient in food and produces great surpluses of dairy produce. Most crops are grown in the southwest. In the north reindeer are herded and forests yield great quantities of lumber for export. Just under 20 per cent of the electricity was supplied by its hydro-electric power stations in the early 1990s. Major industries are lumber products, wood pulp and paper, machinery and shipbuilding, which developed because of the country's great need for an efficient fleet of ice-breakers. Finland has an efficient transport system utilising canals, road, rail and air services.

Quick facts:

Area: 130,559 square miles (338,145 square
    kilometres)
Population: 5,125,000
Capital: Helsinki (Helsingfors)
Other cities: Turku, Tampere
Form of government: Republic
Religion: Lutheranism
Currency: Euro

France

The largest country in western Europe, with a coastline on the English Channel, the Mediterranean Sea and on the Atlantic Ocean. The lowest parts of the country are the great basins of the north and southwest from which it rises to the Massif Central and the higher Alps, Jura and Pyrénées. Climate ranges from moderate maritime in the northwest to Mediterranean in the south. Farming is possible in all parts of France, with forestry and fishing also providing some employment. The western shores are ideal for rearing livestock, while the Paris Basin is good arable land. In the southwest around Bordeaux, vineyards produce some of the world's best wines. The main industrial area of France is in the north and east and the main industries are iron and steel, engineering, chemicals, textiles and electrical goods. France has a long cultural history of art, literature, sculpture and music, and is famous for its immense Gothic churches.

Quick facts:

Area: 212,935 square miles (551,500 square kilometres)
Population: 58,375,000
Capital: Paris
Other cities: Bordeaux, Lyon, Marseille, Nantes, Nice, Toulouse, Strasbourg
Form of government: Republic
Religion: Roman Catholicism
Currency: Euro

French Guiana see GUIANA.

French Polynesia

A total of about 130 islands in the South Pacific Ocean administered as overseas territories by FRANCE. The islands include the Society Islands, the Tuamotu group, the Gambier group, the Tubual Islands and the Marquesas Islands.

Quick facts:

Area: 1,544 square miles (4,000 square kilometres)
Population: 274,000
Capital: Papeete
Form of government: Overseas Territory of France
Religions: Protestantism, Roman Catholicism
Currency: CFP Franc

Gabon

A small country in west central Africa that straddles the equator. It has a low narrow coastal plain and the rest of the country comprises a low plateau. Three-quarters of Gabon is covered by dense tropical forest. The climate is hot, humid and typically equatorial, with little seasonal variation. It was in Lambaréné that Albert Schweitzer, the medical missionary, had his hospital. Until the 1960s lumber was virtually Gabon's only resource and then oil was discovered. By the mid-1980s it was Africa's sixth largest oil producer and other minerals, such as manganese, uranium and iron ore, were being exploited. Deposits of lead and silver have also been discovered. However, around two-thirds of the Gabonese people remain subsistence farmers, growing cassava, sugar cane, plantains and yams. It is believed that the original inhabitants of the country were Pygmies but only a small number of them remain. The country has great tourist potential and as its oil reserves get smaller eco-tourism could become more important to the economy.

Quick facts:
Area: 103,347 square miles (267,668 square kilometres)
Population: 1,424,000
Capital: Libreville
Other major city: Port Gentile
Form of government: Republic
Religions: Roman Catholicism, traditional beliefs
Currency: CFA Franc

Gambia

A small and relatively stable country in Africa, which pokes like a crooked finger into SENEGAL. The country is divided along its entire length by the River Gambia, which can be crossed at only two main ferry crossings. On the coast there are pristine beaches and sand cliffs backed by mangrove swamps, with tropical jungle clothing much of the river banks away from the coast. Gambia has two very different seasons. In the dry season there is little rainfall, then the southwest monsoon sets in, with spectacular storms producing heavy rain for four months. Most Gambians live in villages with a few animals and grow enough millet and sorghum to feed themselves. Groundnuts are the main and only export crop of any significance. The river provides a thriving local fishing industry and the white sandy beaches on the coast are becoming increasingly popular with foreign tourists.

Quick facts:
Area: 4,361 square miles (11,295 square kilometres)
Population: 1,641,000
Capital: Banjul
Form of government: Republic
Religions: Sunni Islam, Christianity
Currency: Dalasi

Georgia

A republic in the southwest of the former USSR, occupying the central and western parts of the Caucasus. It shares borders with TURKEY, ARMENIA, AZERBAIJAN and RUSSIA. It is bounded to the west by the Black Sea. Almost 40 per cent of the country is covered by forests. Agriculture, which is the main occupation of the population, includes tea cultivation and fruit growing, especially citrus fruits and viticulture. The republic is rich in minerals, especially manganese, but has to import the majority of its energy needs. Industries include coal, lumber, machinery, chemicals, silk, food processing and furniture. In the past, the Black Sea tourist trade exploited the country's wealth of thermal and mineral springs very successfully and tourism should again become an economic mainstay. Georgia declared itself independent in 1991. A struggle for regional autonomy by ethnic minorities led to much disruption and violent conflict, and the country lost its access to cheap Soviet energy causing its economy to suffer. In recent years, the US has invested in an oil pipeline from Azerbaijan via Georgia to Turkey and has an increasing influence in the country.

Quick facts:
Area: 26,911 square miles (69,700 square kilometres)
Population: 4,661,000
Capital: T'bilisi
Other cities: Kutaisi, Rustavi, Batumi
Form of government: Republic
Religions: Georgian and Russian Orthodox, Islam
Currency: Lari

Germany

A large populous country in northern central Europe that comprises the former East and West German Republics, unified in 1990. In the north is the North German Plain, which merges with the North Rhinelands in the west. Farther south, a plateau that stretches across the country from east to west is divided by the River Rhine. In the southwest the Black Forest separates the Rhine Valley from the fertile valleys and scarplands of Swabia. More recently, coniferous forests have suffered from acid rain caused by industrial pollution. The Bohemian Uplands and Erz Mountains mark the border with the CZECH REPUBLIC. Generally the country has warm summers and cold winters. Agricultural products include wheat, rye, barley, oats, potatoes and sugar beet, although agriculture accounts for only a small percentage of employment and a third of the country's food has to be imported. The main industrial and most densely populated areas are in the Ruhr Valley. Products of the principal manufacturing industries include iron and steel, motor vehicles, mechanical and electrical equipment, aircraft, ships, computers, electronic and technical goods, chemicals and petrochemicals, pharmaceuticals, textiles, clothing and footwear, foods, beer, optical and high precision instruments.

Quick facts:

Area: 137,735 square miles (356,733 square kilometres)

Population: 82,422,000

Capital: Berlin

Other cities: Bonn, Cologne, Dortmund, Düsseldorf, Essen, Frankfurt, Hamburg, Leipzig, Munich, Stuttgart

Form of government: Federal Republic

Religions: Lutheranism, Roman Catholicism

Currency: Euro

Ghana

A country located on the southern coast of West Africa between CÔTE D'IVOIRE and TOGO. In 1957, as the former British Gold Coast, it became the first black African state to achieve independence from European colonial rule. It has palm-fringed beaches of white sand along the Gulf of Guinea and where the great River Volta meets the sea there are peaceful blue lagoons. The climate on the coast is equatorial and towards the north there are steamy tropical evergreen forests which give way in the far north to tropical savanna. The landscape becomes harsh and barren near the border with BURKINA FASO. Most Ghanaians are village dwellers whose homes are made of locally available materials. The south of the country has been most exposed to European influence and it is here that cocoa, rubber, palm oil and coffee are grown. Ghana's most important crop is cocoa and others include coffee, palm kernels, coconut oil, copra, shea nuts and bananas which are all exported. Fishing is also of major importance and has increased in recent years. Ghana has important mineral resources, notably gold, diamonds, manganese and bauxite. Most of Ghana's towns are in the south.

Quick facts:

Area: 92,100 square miles (238,537 square
   kilometres)
Population: 22,409,000
Capital: Accra
Other cities: Sekondi-Takoradi, Kumasi, Tamale
Form of government: Republic
Religions: Protestantism, traditional beliefs,
   Roman Catholicism, Islam
Currency: Cedi

Gibraltar

A self-governing British Overseas Territory on the southwestern tip of SPAIN, where a limestone hill called the Rock of Gibraltar rises to 1,394 feet (425 metres). Its strategic importance, guarding as it does the western approaches to the Mediterranean and separated from MOROCCO by the narrow Straits of Gibraltar, has resulted in it being occupied at various periods of history by Phoenicians, Carthaginians, Romans, Visigoths, Moors, Spaniards and the British. In 1713, the Treaty of Utrecht awarded Gibraltar to Britain but Spain has never relinquished its claim to the Rock and relations have at times been difficult. English is the official language, although Spanish is also spoken. The British armed forces, tourism, banking and construction are the main sources of employment and most imports are from Britain. The Mediterranean climate and many sites of natural and historical interest attract numerous visitors each year.

Quick facts:
Area: 2.5 square miles (6.5 square kilometres)
Population: 28,000
Capital: Gibraltar
Form of government: Self-governing British
   Overseas Territory
Religion: Christianity
Currency: Gibraltar Pound

Greece

The Greek peninsula is the most southeasterly extension of Europe and has over 1,400 islands lying off its coast and scattered throughout the Aegean Sea. Mainland Greece shares borders with ALBANIA in the northwest, MACEDONIA and BULGARIA in the north and TURKEY in the northeast. The northwestern and central regions of the country are rugged and mountainous, the main chain being the Pindus Mountains. About 70 per cent of the land is hilly, with harsh mountain climates and poor soils and there are few natural resources of economic value although there are deposits of petroleum and natural gas found under the Aegean Sea. The Greek islands and coastal regions have a typical Mediterranean climate, with mild rainy winters and hot dry summers. Winter in the northern mountains is severe, with deep snow and heavy precipitation. About 21 per cent of the people are engaged in agriculture, mostly on small family farms. Forestry and fishing are carried out on a small scale. Greece has undergone a rapid process of industrialisation since the Second World War and pollution is a serious problem in some areas. Tourism is a major source of revenue for the country along with shipping.

Quick facts:
Area: 50,949 square miles (131,957 square
  kilometres)
Population: 10,688,000
Capital: Athens (Athínai)
Other cities: Iráklian, Lárisa, Patras, Piraeus,
  Thessaloníki
Form of government: Republic
Religion: Greek Orthodox
Currency: Euro

Greenland (Kalaallit Nunaat)

The largest island in the world (discounting continental land masses). It lies mainly within the Arctic Circle, off the north-east coast of Canada. Its vast interior is mostly covered with a permanent ice cap that has a known thickness of up to 11,000 feet (3,300 metres). The ice-free coastal strips are characterised by largely barren mountains, rising to Gunnbjorn at 12,140 feet (3,700 metres) in the southeast. Glaciers flow into deeply indented fjords which are fringed by many islands, islets and icebergs. Of the small ice-free fringe, only about a third (58,000 square miles/150,000 square kilometres) can be classed as being inhabited, mainly in the southwest. The largely Inuit population is heavily dependent on fishing for its livelihood, and fish account for 95 per cent of exports. There is some sheep farming and mining of coal and mineral resources as well as iron ore, lead, zinc, uranium and molybdenum.

Quick facts:

Area: 840,000 square miles (2,175,600 square kilometres)

Population: 56,360

Capital: Gothåb (Nuuk)

Form of government: Self-governing Region of Denmark

Religion: Lutheranism

Currency: Danish Krone

Grenada

The most southerly of the Windward Islands chain in the Caribbean and its territory includes the southern Grenadine Islands to the north. The main island consists of the remains of extinct volcanoes and has an attractive wooded landscape. The highest peak is Mount St Catherine at 2,750 feet (838 metres). In the dry season the typical climate is very pleasant, with warm days and cool nights, but in the wet season it is hot day and night. Agriculture is the island's main industry and the chief crops grown for export are citrus fruits, cocoa, nutmegs, bananas and mace. Other crops grown are cloves, cotton, coconuts and cinnamon. Apart from the processing of its crops, Grenada has little manufacturing industry. Tourism is an important source of foreign revenue and Grenada is a popular port of call for cruise ships.

Quick facts:
Area: 133 square miles (344 square kilometres)
Population: 90,000
Capital: St George's
Form of government: Independent State within
  the Commonwealth
Religions: Roman Catholicism, Anglicanism,
  Methodism
Currency: East Caribbean Dollar

Guadeloupe

A small group of islands in the Caribbean lying in the middle of the Lesser Antilles, with some islands in the Leeward Islands and some in the Windward Islands. Since 1946 Guadeloupe has been an overseas department of FRANCE. Ninety per cent of the population live on the two main islands of Basse Terre and Grande Terre. Basse Terre is mountainous, covered with rainforest and dominated by the Soufrière volcano at 4,318 feet (1,467 metres). Grande Terre is flat and dry with white sandy beaches. The other islands include Marie Galante, La Désirade, Iles des Saints, St Barthélémy and St Martin. Guadeloupe is susceptible to earthquakes and hurricanes. The islands have a warm and humid climate with rainfall heaviest between May and November. Main exports include bananas, sugar and rum. Tourism is important and the country is a port of call for cruise ships.

Quick facts:

Area: 658 square miles (1,705 square kilometres)
Population: 431,000
Capital: Basse Terre
Other main town: Pointe-à-Pitre
Form of government: French Overseas Department
Religion: Roman Catholicism
Currency: Euro

Guam

Guam is the most southerly and the largest of the Mariana Islands in the northwest Pacific. It consists mainly of a high, coraline limestone plateau with some low volcanic mountains in the south of the island. Guam's climate is tropical with a rainy season from July to December. An unincorporated territory of the USA, its economy depends to a large extent on government activities and military installations account for some 35 per cent of the land area of the island. Exports include copra, palm oil and processed fish. The country has also become a financial centre, particularly for mainland and Asian banks, and tourism has come to play an important role in its economy.

Quick facts:
Area: 212 square miles (549 square kilometres)
Population: 171,000
Capital: Agana
Form of government: Unincorporated Territory of the USA
Religion: Roman Catholicism
Currency: US Dollar

Guatemala

A country situated between the Pacific Ocean and the Caribbean Sea where North America meets Central America. It is mountainous, with a ridge of volcanoes running parallel to the Pacific coast. It has a tropical climate with little or no variation in temperature and a distinctive wet season. The Pacific slopes of the mountains are exceptionally well watered and fertile and it is here that most of the population is settled. Coffee-growing on the lower slopes dominates the economy, although bananas, sugar, cardamom, petroleum and shellfish are exported. The forested area of the country, about 36 per cent, plays an important part in the country's economy and produces balsam, cabinet woods, chicle and oils. There are also deposits of petroleum and zinc, while lead and silver are mined. Industry is mainly restricted to the processing of the agricultural products. Guatemala is politically a very unstable country and civil conflict over a period of 36 years has left the country impoverished and at the mercy of organised crime and drug-trafficking.

Quick facts:

Area: 42,042 square miles (108,889 square
   kilometres)
Population: 12,293,000
Capital: Guatemala City
Other cities: Cobán, Puerto Barrios,
   Quezaltenango
Form of government: Republic
Religion: Roman Catholicism
Currency: Quetzal/US Dollar

Guiana (French) or Guyane

Situated on the northeast coast of South America and still an overseas department of FRANCE, Guiana is bounded to the south and east by BRAZIL and to the west by SURINAM. The climate is tropical with heavy rainfall. Guiana's economy relies almost completely on subsidies from France. It has little to export apart from shrimps and the small area of land that is cultivated produces rice, manioc and sugar cane. Recently the French have tried to develop the tourist industry and exploit the extensive reserves of hardwood in the jungle interior. This has led to a growing sawmill industry and the export of logs. Natural resources, in addition to lumber, include bauxite, cinnabar (mercury ore) and gold (although this is in scattered deposits). The Ariane rocket launch site of the European Space Agency is located at Kourou.

Quick facts:
Area: 34,749 square miles (90,000 square kilometres)
Population: 199,000
Capital: Cayenne
Form of government: French Overseas Department
Religion: Roman Catholicism
Currency: Euro

Guinea

Formerly a French West African territory, Guinea is located on the coast at the 'bulge' in Africa. It is a lush green beautiful country about the same size as the UNITED KINGDOM. It has a tropical climate with constant heat and a high rainfall near the coast. Its principal rivers are the Gambia and the Bafing while the Niger rises in the forests of the Guinea Highlands. Guinea has great agricultural potential and many of the coastal swamps and forested plains have been cleared for the cultivation of rice, cassava, yams, maize and vegetables. Around 80 per cent of the population are subsistence farmers. Farther inland, on the plateau of Fouta Djallon, dwarf cattle are raised and in the valleys bananas and pineapples are grown. Coffee and kola nuts are important cash crops grown in the Guinea Highlands to the southwest. Minerals such as bauxite, of which there are substantial reserves, iron ore, diamonds, gold and uranium are mined. However, economic development and stability are now hampered by the presence of refugees from the fighting in Sierra Leone and Liberia and ongoing economic mismanagement.

Quick facts:

Area: 94,926 square miles (245,857 square kilometres)
Population: 9,690,000
Capital: Conakry
Other cities: Kankan, Kindia, Labé
Form of government: Republic
Religion: Sunni Islam
Currency: Guinean Franc

Guinea-Bissau

Formerly a Portuguese territory but granted independence in 1974, Guinea-Bissau is located south of SENEGAL on the Atlantic coast of West Africa. The republic's territory includes over 60 coastal islands, including the archipelago of Bijagós. It is a country of stunning scenery and rises from a deeply indented and island-fringed coastline to a low inland plateau and hills on the border with neighbouring GUINEA. The climate is tropical, with abundant rain from June to November but hot dry conditions for the rest of the year. The country's main aim is to become self-sufficient in food and the main crops grown by the subsistence farmers are rice, groundnuts, cassava, sugar cane, plantains, maize and co-conuts. Fishing is an important export industry although cashew nuts are the principal export. Peanuts, palm products and cotton are also a source of export revenue. Years of Portuguese rule and civil war have left Guinea-Bissau impoverished. With massive foreign debt, it is one of the poorest West African states and political instability continues to adversely affect the economy.

Quick facts:
Area: 13,948 square miles (36,125 square
   kilometres)
Population: 1,442,000
Capital: Bissau
Form of government: Republic
Religions: Traditional beliefs, Sunni Islam
Currency: CFA Franc

Guyana

The only English-speaking country in South America, situated on the northeast coast of the continent on the Atlantic Ocean. Guyana was formerly called British Guiana but achieved independence in 1966. The country is intersected by many rivers and the coastal area comprises tidal marshes and mangrove swamps. It is on this narrow coastal area that rice is grown and vast plantations produce sugar. The jungle in the southwest has potential for the production of minerals, hardwood and hydroelectric power, but 90 per cent of the population live in the coastal area where the climate is moderated by sea breezes. Sugar and its by-products and rice are the mainstay of the country's economy, while tropical fruits and vegetables, such as coconuts, citrus, coffee and corn, are grown mainly for home consumption. Large numbers of livestock including cattle, sheep, pigs and chickens are also raised. Guyana's principal mineral is bauxite, with gold, manganese and diamonds also being produced. It remains among the region's poorest countries due to political instability, racial tension between the two main population groups and poor economic management.

Quick facts:

Area: 83,000 square miles (214,969 square kilometres)
Population: 767,000
Capital: Georgetown
Other cities: Linden, New Amsterdam
Form of government: Cooperative Republic
Religions: Hinduism, Protestantism, Roman Catholicism, Islam
Currency: Guyanese Dollar

Guyane see GUIANA.

Haiti

Occupying the western third of the large island of Hispaniola in the Caribbean, Haiti is a mountainous country consisting of five different ranges, the highest point reaching 8,793 feet (2,680 metres) at Pic La Selle. The mountain ranges are separated by deep valleys and plains. The climate is tropical but semi-arid conditions can occur in the lee of the central mountains. Hurricanes and severe thunderstorms are a common occurrence. Only a third of the country is arable, yet agriculture is the chief occupation, with around 80 per cent of the population concentrated in rural areas. Many farmers grow enough to feed only their own families, and the export crops of coffee, sugar and sisal are grown on large estates. Severe soil erosion caused by extensive forest clearance has resulted in a decline in crop yields and environmental damage has been caused. The country has only limited amounts of natural resources, bauxite not now being commercially profitable, although deposits of salt, copper and gold exist. Haiti is the poorest country in the Americas and has experienced many uprisings and attempted coups.

Quick facts:
Area: 10,714 square miles (27,750 square kilometres)
Population: 8,308,000
Capital: Port-au-Prince
Other towns: Cap-Haïtien, Les Cayes, Gonaïves
Form of government: Republic
Religions: Roman Catholicism, Voodooism
Currency: Gourde

Honduras

A fan-shaped country in Central America that spreads out towards the Caribbean Sea at the Gulf of Honduras. Four-fifths of the country is covered by mountains that are indented with river valleys running towards the very short Pacific coast. There is little change in temperatures throughout the year and rainfall is heavy, especially on the Caribbean coast where temperatures are also higher than inland. The highlands are covered with forests, mainly of oak and pine, while palms and mangroves grow in the coastal areas. The country is sparsely populated and, although agricultural, only about 25 per cent of the land is cultivated. Honduras was once the world's leading banana exporter and although that fruit is still its main export, agriculture is now more diverse. Grains, coffee and sugar are important crops, and these are grown mainly on the coastal plains of the Pacific and Caribbean. Forestry is one of the principal industries, producing mahogany, pine, walnut, ebony and rosewood. However, Honduras remains one of the least developed countries in the region due to military rule, crime and natural disasters such as Hurricane Mitch in 1998.

Quick facts:
Area: 43,277 square miles (112,088 square
   kilometres)
Population: 7,326,000
Capital: Tegucigalpa
Other cities: San Pedro Sula, La Ceiba, Puerto
   Cortès
Form of government: Republic
Religion: Roman Catholicism
Currency: Lempira

Hong Kong

Formerly a British Dependent Territory, on 1 July 1997 it became a Special Administrative Region of China. Hong Kong is located in the South China Sea and consists of Hong Kong Island (once a barren rock), the peninsula of Kowloon and about 386 square miles (1,000 square kilometres) of adjacent land known as the New Territories. Hong Kong is situated at the mouth of the Pearl River, about 81 miles (130 kilometres) southeast of Guangzhou (Canton). The climate is warm subtropical with cool dry winters and hot humid summers. Hong Kong has no natural resources, even its water comes from reservoirs across the Chinese border. Its main assets are its magnificent natural harbour and its position close to the main trading routes of the Pacific. Hong Kong's economy is based on free enterprise and trade, an industrious work force and an efficient and aggressive commercial system. Hong Kong's main industries are textiles, clothing, tourism and electronics.

Quick facts:
Area: 415 square miles (1,075 square
  kilometres)
Population: 6,940,200
Form of government: Special Administrative
  Region of China
Religions: Buddhism, Taoism, Christianity
Currency: Hong Kong Dollar

Hungary

Landlocked in the heartland of Europe, Hungary is dominated by the great plain to the east of the River Danube, which runs north-south across the country, its tributaries including the Tisza, the longest river. In the west lies the largest lake in Central Europe, Lake Balaton. Winters are severe, but the summers are warm and although wet in the west, summer droughts often occur in the east. Agricultural produce includes wheat, maize, sunflower seed, potatoes, pigs, cattle, poultry and dairy products. Even prior to the collapse of communism in the country, the government was moving to a free market economy. Industries have been carefully developed where adequate natural resources exist, such as bauxite, which is the country's main resource. Industries include mining, metallurgy, construction materials, processed foods, pharmaceuticals and motor vehicles. Tourism is also an important industry. Foreign investment is high and in 2004 the country became a member of the European Union.

Quick facts:
Area: 35,920 square miles (93,032 square
  kilometres)
Population: 9,981,000
Capital: Budapest
Other cities: Debrecen, Miskolc, Pécs, Szeged
Form of government: Parliamentary Democracy
Religions: Roman Catholicism, Calvinism,
  Lutheranism
Currency: Forint

Iceland

A large island situated in a tectonically unstable part of the North Atlantic Ocean, just south of the Arctic Circle. The island has over 100 volcanoes, at least one of which erupts every five years. One-ninth of the country is covered by ice and snow fields, and there are about 700 hot springs, which are an important source of central heating, particularly in the volcanic areas. In the capital city, the majority of homes and industries are heated by this method. The climate is cool temperate, but because of the effect of the North Atlantic Drift it is mild for its latitude. Permanent daylight occurs for three months in summer and the beautiful Aurora Borealis (Northern Lights) can be seen from the end of August. The southwest corner is the most densely populated area as the coast here is generally free from ice. Very little of the land can be cultivated and the main crops are root vegetables such as turnip and potatoes. Fishing and fish processing are the mainstay of the Icelandic economy, with much of the catch being exported. Aluminium and ferrosilicon, nitrates for fertilisers, cement and chemicals are produced for export. Other manufactured goods include paints, textiles, clothing, footwear and knitted products. Tourism is also of growing importance to the island.

Quick facts:

Area: 39,769 square miles (103,000 square kilometres)
Population: 299,300
Capital: Reykjavík
Other cities: Akureyri, Kópavogur
Form of government: Republic
Religion: Lutheranism
Currency: Icelandic Króna

India

A vast country in South Asia that is dominated in the extreme north by the world's youngest and highest mountains, the Himalayas, which extend about 1,500 miles (about 2,400 kilometres) along India's northern and eastern borders. The range contains Mount Everest and K2. At the foot of the Himalayas, a huge plain, drained by the Indus and Ganges rivers, is one of the most fertile areas in the world and the most densely populated part of India. Farther south the ancient Deccan plateau extends to the southern tip of the country. India generally has four seasons, the cool, the hot, the rainy and the dry. About 70 per cent of the population depend on agriculture for their living and the lower slopes of the Himalayas represent one of the world's best tea-growing areas. Rice, sugar cane and wheat are grown in the Ganges plain, and there is a comprehensive system of irrigation to aid agriculture. India is self-sufficient in all its major food crops and main exports include precious stones, jewellery, engineering products, clothes and chemicals. India has been troubled by internal dissent and external disputes, particularly with Pakistan over the status of Kashmir, but in recent years it has encouraged foreign investment and its economy is benefitting in particular from its skills in the field of information technology.

Quick facts:

Area: 1,269,346 square miles (3,287,590
   square kilometres)
Population: 1,095,350,000
Capital: New Delhi
Other cities: Ahmadabad, Bangalore, Bombay,
   Calcutta, Delhi, Madras, Hyderabad, Kanpur
Form of government: Federal Republic
Religions: Hinduism, Islam, Sikkism,
   Christianity, Jainism, Buddhism
Currency: Indian Rupee

Indonesia

A country made up of 13,667 islands that are scattered across the Indian and Pacific Oceans in a huge crescent. It is the world's fourth most highly populated country. Its largest landmass is the province of Kalimantan, which is part of the island of Borneo. Sumatra is the largest individual island. Java, however, is the dominant and most densely populated island. The climate is generally tropical monsoon and temperatures are high all year round. The country has 130 active volcanoes and earthquakes are frequent in the southern islands. The tsunami of December 2004, triggered by an underground earthquake off the coast of Sumatra, caused much devastation, especially in the province of Aceh. Rice, maize and cassava are the main crops grown. Indonesia has the largest reserves of tin in the world and is one of the world's leading rubber producers. Other mineral resources found are bauxite, natural gas, nickel and copper. Oil production is also important. Indonesia's resources are not as yet fully developed but the development of the country's economy has been hampered by the devastation caused by the 2004 tsunami as well as ongoing political instability, corruption, human rights violations and armed separatist movements in Aceh and Papua.

Quick facts:

Area: 735,358 square miles (1,904,569 square kilometres)

Population: 245,452,000

Capital: Jakarta

Other cities: Bandung, Medan, Palembang, Semarang, Surabaya

Form of government: Republic

Religions: Sunni Islam, Christianity, Hinduism

Currency: Indonesian Rupiah

Iran, Islamic Republic of

Lying across The Gulf from the Arabian Peninsula and stretching from the Caspian Sea to the Arabian Sea, Iran is a land dominated by mountains in the north and west, with a huge expanse of desert in its centre. The climate is hot and dry, although more temperate conditions are found on the shores of the Caspian Sea. In winter, terrible dust storms sweep the deserts and almost no life can survive. Most of the population live in the north and west, where Tehran is situated. The only good agricultural land is on the Caspian coastal plains, where wheat, barley, potatoes and rice are grown. Fresh and dried fruit are the country's main exports apart from petroleum. About 5 per cent of the population are nomadic herdsmen who wander in the mountains. Most of Iran's oil is in the southwest, and other valuable minerals include coal, iron ore, copper and lead. Precious stones are found in the northeast. Main exports are petrochemicals, carpets and rugs, textiles, raw cotton and leather goods. There was a rapid expansion in the economy from petroleum industry revenue. After the Islamic revolution in the late 1970s, however, and war with Iraq, the economy slowed dramatically and is only gradually beginning to pick up again.

Quick facts:
Area: 634,293 square miles (1,648,195 square kilometres)
Population: 68,688,000
Capital: Tehran
Other cities: Esfahan, Mashhad, Tabriz
Form of government: Islamic Republic
Religion: Shia Islam
Currency: Iranian Rial

Iraq

Located in southwest Asia, wedged between The Gulf and Syria, Iraq is almost landlocked except for its outlet to the Gulf at Shatt al Arab. Its two great rivers, the Tigris and the Euphrates, flow from the northwest into the Gulf at this point. The climate is arid, with very hot summers and cold winters. The high mountains on the border with TURKEY are snow-covered for six months of the year, and desert in the southwest covers nearly half the country. The only fertile land in Iraq is in the basins of the Tigris and Euphrates, where wheat, barley, rice, tobacco and cotton are grown, with the country being primarily an agricultural one. Iraq profited from the great oil boom of the 1970s, but during the war with Iran, oil terminals in the Gulf were destroyed and the Trans-Syrian Pipeline closed. Iraq invaded Kuwait in 1990, leading to the Gulf War in 1991 in which Iraq was defeated by United Nation forces. In a state of economic crisis since then, the regime of Saddam Hussein, President since 1979, collapsed in April 2003, three weeks into a major US-led military campaign. Unity government and US-led coalition forces still remain in Iraq amid ongoing violence to facilitate the restoration of security and order.

Quick facts:
Area: 169,235 square miles (438,317 square
    kilometres)
Population: 26,783,000
Capital: Baghdad
Other cities: Al-Basrah, Al Mawsil
Form of government: Republic
Religions: Shia Islam, Sunni Islam
Currency: New Iraqi Dinar

Ireland, Republic of

One of Europe's most westerly countries, situated in the Atlantic Ocean and separated from Great Britain by the Irish Sea. It has an equable climate, with mild southwest winds, which makes temperatures uniform over most of the country. The Republic extends over four-fifths of the island of Ireland and the west and southwest are mountainous, with the highest peak reaching 3,416 feet (1,041 metres) at Carrauntoohil. The central plain is largely limestone covered by boulder clay, which provides good farmland and pasture with about 80 per cent of the land being under agriculture. The main rivers are the Erne and the Shannon. Livestock production is the most important, including cattle, sheep, pigs and horses. The rural population have tended to migrate to the cities, mainly Dublin, which is the main industrial centre and the focus of radio, television, publishing and communications. Lack of energy resources and remoteness from major markets did slow industrial development, but by taking full advantage of membership of the European Union the economy has improved markedly in recent years, particularly tourism.

Quick facts:

Area: 27,137 square miles (70,284 square kilometres)

Population: 4,062,000

Capital: Dublin (Baile Atha Cliath)

Other cities: Cork, Galway, Limerick, Waterford

Form of government: Republic

Religion: Roman Catholicism

Currency: Euro

World Facts

Israel

Occupying a long narrow stretch of land in the southeast of the Mediterranean, Israel's eastern boundary is formed by the Great Rift Valley through which the River Jordan flows to the Dead Sea. The south of the country is made up of a triangular wedge of the Negev desert, which ends at the Gulf of Aqaba. The Negev desert has mineral resources, such as copper, phosphates and manganese, plus commercial amounts of natural gas and petroleum. Other assets are the vast amounts of potash, bromine and other minerals found in the Dead Sea. The climate in summer is hot and dry; in winter it is mild with some rain. The south of the country is arid and barren. Most of the population live on the coastal plain bordering the Mediterranean where Tel Aviv (Tel Aviv-Yafo) is the country's main commercial centre. Israel's agriculture is based on collective settlements known as kibbutz. The country is virtually self-sufficient in foodstuffs and a major exporter of its produce. A wide range of products is processed or finished in the country and main exports include finished diamonds, textiles, fruit, vegetables, chemicals, machinery and fertilisers. Tourism also makes an important contribution to the economy. Israel's uneasy relationship with Palestinian nationals in the West Bank and Gaza Strip territories often flares up into open conflict in the region.

Quick facts:
Area: 8,130 square miles (21,056 square
  kilometres)
Population: 6,352,000
Capital: UN recognised capital Tel Aviv/
  Jerusalem
Other cities: Haifa
Form of government: Parliamentary Democracy
Religions: Judaism, Sunni Islam, Christianity
Currency: New Israeli Shekel

Italy

A republic in southern Europe that comprises a large peninsula and the two main islands of Sicily and Sardinia. The Alps form a natural boundary with its northern and western European neighbours and the Adriatic Sea to the east separates it from the countries of former YUGOSLAVIA. The Apennine Mountains form the backbone of Italy and extend the full length of the peninsula. Between the Alps and the Apennines lies the Po Valley, a great fertile lowland. Sicily and Sardinia are largely mountainous. Much of Italy is geologically unstable and it has four active volcanoes, including Etna, Vesuvius AND Stromboli. Italy enjoys warm dry summers and mild winters. In the south farms are small and traditional. Industries in the north include motor vehicles, textiles, clothing, leather goods, glass and ceramics. Although there is a lack of natural resources, almost 60 per cent of the land is under crops and pasture and there is an abundance of building stone, particularly marble. The coastal waters are rich in marine life, with anchovy, sardine and tuna being of commercial importance. Tourism is an important source of foreign currency.

Quick facts:
Area: 116,320 square miles (301,268 square
   kilometres)
Population: 58,133,000
Capital: Rome (Roma)
Other cities: Milan, Naples, Turin, Genoa,
   Palermo, Florence
Form of government: Republic
Religion: Roman Catholicism
Currency: Euro

Jamaica

An island state in the Caribbean Sea about 93 miles (150 kilometres) south of CUBA. The centre of the island comprises a limestone plateau and this is surrounded by narrow coastal flatlands and palm-fringed beaches. The highest mountains, the Blue Mountains, are in the east of the island. The climate is tropical, with high temperatures at the coast and slightly cooler and less humid conditions in the highlands. Jamaica suffers from severe earthquakes and thermal springs can be found in areas of the country. The island lies right in the middle of the hurricane zone. The traditional crops grown are sugar cane, bananas, peppers, ginger, cocoa and coffee and new crops such as winter vegetables, fruit and honey are being developed for export. The mining of bauxite and alumina plays a very important part in Jamaica's economy and accounts for around 60 per cent of its total yearly exports. Industrialisation has been encouraged and clothing, footwear, cement and agricultural machinery are now produced. Despite the country's relative stability, widespread poverty still exists. Tourism is a particularly important industry, with over one million visitors annually, but its success is threatened by ongoing lawlessness in the country.

Quick facts:
Area: 4,243 square miles (10,990 square
  kilometres)
Population: 2,758,000
Capital: Kingston
Other town: Montego Bay
Form of government: Parliamentary Democracy
Religions: Anglicanism, Roman Catholicism,
  Protestantism
Currency: Jamaican Dollar

Japan

Located on the eastern margin of Asia and consisting of four major islands, Honshu, Hokkaido, Kyushu and Shikoku and many small islands, Japan is separated from the mainland of Asia by the Sea of Japan. The country is made up of six chains of steep serrated mountains, which contain about 60 active volcanoes. Earthquakes are frequent and widespread and often accompanied by giant waves (tsunami). A devastating earthquake occurred in 1995 when more than 5,000 people died and over 300,000 were left homeless. Summers are warm and humid and winters mild, except on Hokkaido, which is covered in snow in winter. Japan's agriculture is highly advanced, with extensive use made of fertilisers and miniature machinery for the small fields. Fishing is very important, both for domestic consumption and export. Heavy industries, such as iron and steel, shipbuilding, chemicals and petrochemicals, used to account for almost three-quarters of Japan's export revenue, but now it has to rely on the success of its manufacturing industry which produces automobiles, televisions, videos, electronic equipment, cameras, watches, clocks, robots and textiles. Japan's financial markets have experienced some problems in recent years, which has introduced some uncertainty into what was a very secure economy.

Quick facts:

Area: 145,870 square miles (377,801 square
   kilometres)
Population: 127,463,000
Capital: Tokyo
Other cities: Osaka, Nagoya, Sapporo, Kobe,
   Kyoto, Yokohama
Form of government: Constitutional Monarchy
Religions: Shintoism, Buddhism, Christianity
Currency: Yen

Jordan

Almost landlocked except for a short coastline on the Gulf of Aqaba, Jordan is bounded by SAUDI ARABIA, SYRIA, IRAQ and ISRAEL. Almost 80 per cent of the country is desert and the rest comprises the East Bank Uplands and Jordan Valley, part of the Great Rift Valley. In general, summers are hot and dry and winters cool and wet, with variations related to altitude. The east has a desert climate. Since under 5 per cent of the land is arable and only part of this is irrigated, production of grain is insufficient for the country's needs although some fruits and vegetables are grown for export. The capital, Amman, is the main industrial centre of the country and the industries include phosphates, petroleum products, cement, iron and fertilisers. The rich Arab states such as Saudi Arabia give Jordan substantial economic aid and the country has a modern network of roads that link the cities. In 1994 an historic peace agreement was signed with Israel that ended 46 years of hostilities.

Quick facts:
Area: 37,738 square miles (97,740 square
   kilometres)
Population: 5,906,000
Capital: Amman
Other cities: Aqaba, Irbid, Zarqa
Form of government: Constitutional Monarchy
Religion: Sunni Islam
Currency: Jordanian Dinar

Kazakhstan

The second largest republic of the former USSR, which extends from the coast of the Caspian Sea to the northwest corner of MONGOLIA. The west of the country is low-lying, the east hilly and in the southeast mountainous areas include parts of the Tian Shan and Altai ranges. The climate is continental and very dry, with great extremes of temperature. Much of the country is desert and semi-desert, with wastelands of stone, sand and salt. Crops can be grown only in the wetter northwest regions or on land irrigated by the Syrdar'ya river. Extensive pastoral farming is carried out and cattle, sheep and goats are the main livestock reared. The country is rich in minerals, particularly copper, lead, zinc, coal, tungsten, iron ore, oil and gas. Kazakhstan declared itself independent in 1991, since when economic prospects have remained positive, although environmental problems have been left as a legacy of past Soviet exploitation and have still to be tackled (e.g. the overdraining of the Aral Sea). Parts of the country, particularly the mountainous regions, are subject to earthquakes and the former capital, Almaty, has been largely rebuilt following extensive damage. In 1997 the capital was moved to Astana, located in a more stable geological region.

Quick facts:

Area: 1,049,156 square miles (2,717,300 square kilometres)
Population: 15,671,000
Capital: Astana
Other major city: Almaty
Form of government: Republic
Religion: Sunni Islam, Russian Orthodox
Currency: Tenge

Kenya

Located in East Africa, Kenya straddles the equator and extends from Lake Victoria in the southwest to the Indian Ocean in the southeast. Highlands run north to south through central Kenya and are divided by the steep-sided Great Rift Valley. The coastal lowlands have a hot humid climate but in the highlands it is cooler and rainfall heavier. In the east it is very arid. The southwestern region is well watered, with huge areas of fertile soil and this accounts for the bulk of the population and almost all its economic production. A wide variety of crops are grown for domestic consumption, such as wheat, maize and cassava. Tea, coffee, sisal, sugar cane and cotton are grown for export. Oil refining at Mombasa is the country's largest single industry and other industry includes food processing and textiles. Mining is carried out on a small scale for soda ash, gold and limestone, but large quantities of silver and lead exist near Mombasa. Tourism is an important source of foreign revenue, the many wildlife and game reserves being a major attraction.

Quick facts:

Area: 224,081 square miles (580,367 square kilometres)
Population: 34,707,000
Capital: Nairobi
Other cities: Mombasa, Eldoret, Kisumu, Nakuru
Form of government: Republic
Religions: Roman Catholicism, Protestantism, other Christianity, traditional beliefs
Currency: Kenyan Shilling

Kiribati

Formerly known as the Gilbert and Ellice Islands, Kiribati comprises three groups of coral atolls and one isolated volcanic island spread over a large expanse of the central Pacific Ocean. The group includes the former Gilbert Islands, the Phoenix Islands (now Rawaki) and the southern Line Islands. The largest island is Kiritimati, formerly known as Christmas Island. The climate is maritime equatorial, with a rainy season from October to March. Most islanders are involved in subsistence agriculture. The principal tree is the coconut, which grows well on all the islands. There are palm and breadfruit trees and bananas and papaws to be found. Tuna fishing is an important industry, with coconuts and palm products being the main cash crops. Ocean Island (Banaba) was a rich source of phosphate deposits (guano) but these are now exhausted and the mining has left severe environmental damage, causing most Banabans to resettle elsewhere. Tourism is becoming increasingly important but the country is heavily dependent on overseas aid.

Quick facts:
Area: 280 square miles (726 square kilometres)
Population: 85,000
Capital: Tarawa
Form of government: Republic
Religions: Roman Catholicism, Protestantism
Currency: Australian Dollar

Korea, Democratic People's Republic of (North Korea)

A country occupying the northern half of the Korean peninsula in east Asia and formerly known as North Korea. The Yala and Tumen rivers form its northern border with CHINA and RUSSIA. Its southern border with the Republic of KOREA is just north of the 38th parallel. It is a mountainous country, three-quarters of which is forested highland or scrubland, with Paektu-San the highest peak at 9,003 feet (2,737 metres). The climate is warm temperate, although winters can be cold in the north. Most rain falls during the summer. Nearly 90 per cent of its arable land is farmed by cooperatives that employ over 40 per cent of the labour force and rice is the main crop grown. North Korea is quite well endowed with fuel and minerals such as magnesite, zinc, copper, lead, tungsten, gold and silver. Deposits of coal and hydroelectric power generate electricity and substantial deposits of iron ore are found near Pyongyang and Musan. Sixty per cent of the labour force is employed in industry, the most important of which are metallurgical, building, cement and chemicals. Fishing is carried on, with the main catches being tuna, anchovy and seaweeds. North Korea has maintained a very isolationist policy and the country has experienced acute food shortages caused by natural disasters and poor economic management.

Quick facts:
Area: 46,540 square miles (120,538 square kilometres)
Population: 23,113,000
Capital: Pyongyang
Other cities: Chongjin, Wonsan, Hamhung
Form of government: Socialist Republic
Religions: Buddhism, Confucianism
Currency: North Korean Won

Korea, Republic of (South Korea)

Formerly South Korea, the country occupies the southern half of the Korean peninsula in eastern Asia. It is bordered in the north by a demilitarised zone which acts as a buffer between the former South and North Koreas. Most of the country is hilly or mountainous, with the highest ranges running north to south along the east coast. The west is lowland and extremely densely populated. The extreme south has a humid warm temperate climate while farther north it is more continental. Most rain falls in summer. Cultivated land represents only 23 per cent of the country's total area and the main crops are rice, onions, potatoes, barley and maize. An increasing amount of fruit, such as melons, apples and peaches, is now produced. The country has few natural resources but does produce coal, graphite and iron ore. It has a flourishing manufacturing industry and is the world's leading supplier of ships and footwear. Other important industries are electronic equipment, electrical goods, steel, petrochemicals, motor vehicles and toys. Its people enjoy a much higher standard of living than their northern neighbours as a result of the country's transformation into one of the world's major economies.

Quick facts:

Area: 38,368 square miles (99,373 square kilometres)
Population: 48,846,000
Capital: Seoul (Soul)
Other cities: Pusan, Taegu
Form of government: Republic
Religions: Buddhism, Christianity, Confucianism
Currency: South Korean Won

Kuwait

A tiny Arab state on The Gulf, comprising the city of Kuwait at the southern entrance of Kuwait Bay, a small undulating desert wedged between IRAQ and SAUDI ARABIA and nine small offshore islands. It has a dry desert climate, cool in winter but very hot and humid in summer. There is little agriculture because of lack of water. The major crops produced are melons, tomatoes, onions and dates. The country's water comes from the desalination of seawater. Shrimp fishing is becoming an important industry. Large reserves of petroleum and natural gas are the mainstay of the economy. Apart from oil, industries includes boat-building, plastics, petrochemicals, gases, cement and building materials. Kuwait was invaded by Iraq in 1990 before a US-led campaign drove out the Iraqi forces the following year. In recent years, Kuwait has provided an important transit route for forces and civilians moving in and out of war-torn Iraq.

Quick facts:
Area: 6,880 square miles (17,818 square kilometres)
Population: 2,418,000
Capital: Kuwait City (Al Kuwayt)
Government: Constitutional Hereditary Emirate
Religions: Sunni Islam, Shia Islam
Currency: Kuwaiti Dinar

Kyrgyzstan

A central Asian republic of the former USSR, independent since 1991. It is located on the border with northwest CHINA. Much of the country is occupied by the Tian Shan Mountains, which rise to spectacular peaks. The highest is Pik Pobedy at 24,406 feet (7,439 metres), lying on the border with China. In the northeast of the country is Issyk Kul, a large lake heated by volcanic action, so it never freezes in winter. Most of the country is semi-arid or desert, but climate is greatly influenced by altitude. Soils are badly leached except in the valleys, where some grains are grown. Grazing of sheep, horses and cattle is extensive. Industries include non-ferrous metallurgy, machine building, coal mining, tobacco, food processing, textiles, gold mining and hydroelectricity. The country has large mineral deposits of gold, coal and uranium, while deposits of natural gas and oil have not, as yet, been developed. Parts of Kyrgyzstan are threatened by environmental pollution caused by storage of toxic waste and radioactive material which are the by-products of mining, former nuclear tests and the overuse of chemicals, especially fertilisers. The government is making efforts to address this problem and encourage foreign visitors.

Quick facts:

Area: 76,641 square miles (198,500 square kilometres)
Population: 5,213,000
Capital: Bishkek
Other major city: Osh
Form of government: Republic
Religions: Sunni Islam, Russian Orthodox
Currency: Som

Laos

A landlocked country in Southeast Asia that is ruggedly mountainous, apart from the Mekong river plains along its border with THAILAND. The Annam Mountains, which reach 8,203 feet (2,500 metres), form a natural border with VIETNAM. It has a tropical monsoon climate, with high temperatures throughout the year and heavy rains in summer. Laos is one of the poorest countries in the world and its development has been retarded by war, drought and floods. It is primarily an agricultural country, with rice being the principal crop grown on small peasant plots. The mighty Mekong river provides the main means of transport as well as irrigation for the rice paddies upon which the people's subsistence depends. Corn, potatoes and cassava are also grown. There is some export of lumber, coffee, tin and electricity. All manufactured goods must be imported and are mainly food, machinery, petroleum products and electrical equipment. The capital and largest city, Vientiane, is the country's main trade outlet via Thailand.

Quick facts:

Area: 91,429 square miles (236,800 square kilometres)

Population: 6,368,000

Capital: Vientiane

Other cities: Luang Prabang, Savannakhét, Paksé

Form of government: People's Democratic Republic

Religions: Buddhism, traditional beliefs

Currency: Kip

Latvia

A Baltic state that regained its independence in 1991 with the break-up of the former Soviet Union. It is located in northeast Europe on the Baltic Sea and is sandwiched between ESTONIA and LITHUANIA. It has cool summers, wet summers and long, cold winters. Latvians traditionally lived by forestry, fishing and livestock rearing. The chief agricultural occupations are cattle and dairy farming and the main crops grown are oats, barley, rye, potatoes and flax. Latvia's population is now over 70 per cent urban and agriculture is no longer the mainstay of the economy. It has a well-developed industrial base and produces electric railway carriages, electronic and electrical equipment (radios and refrigerators), paper, cement, chemicals, textiles, woolen goods, furniture and foodstuffs. Latvia has abundant deposits of peat and gypsum but lacks other fossil fuels and minerals, which has made it heavily dependent on imports of oil, gas and electricity. Hydroelectric plants on the Daugava river supply over half of the domestic production of electricity, which in total amounts to about 50 per cent of overall consumption. Economic development was difficult in the years following independence but the situation is gradually improving. Latvia became a member of the European Union in 2004.

Quick facts:
Area: 24,942 square miles (64,600 square
  kilometres)
Population: 2,274,000
Capital: Riga
Other cities: Liepaja, Daugavpils
Form of government: Republic
Religions: Lutheranism, Roman Catholicism,
  Russian Orthodox
Currency: Latvian Lat

Lebanon

A mountainous country in the eastern Mediterranean. A narrow coastal plain runs parallel to its 149-mile (240-kilometre) Mediterranean coast and gradually rises to the spectacular Lebanon Mountains, which are snow-covered in winter. The Anti-Lebanon Mountains form the border with SYRIA and between the two ranges lies the Beqaa Valley. The climate is Mediterranean, with short warm winters and long hot and rainless summers. Rainfall can be torrential in winter and snow falls on high ground. Lebanon is an agricultural country, the main regions of production being the Beqaa Valley and the coastal plain, although erosion is a common problem in the uplands. Main products include olives, grapes, bananas, citrus fruits, apples, cotton, tobacco and sugar beet. Industry is small scale and manufactures include cement, fertilisers and jewellery. There are oil refineries at Tripoli and Sidon. Lebanon's main economy is based on commercial services such as banking, but civil war, invasion by Israel and factional fighting have created severe problems for the economy, causing high inflation and unemployment.

Quick facts:
Area: 4,015 square miles (10,400 square
    kilometres)
Population: 3,874,000
Capital: Beirut (Beyrouth)
Other major cities: Tripoli, Sidon
Form of government: Republic
Religions: Shia Islam, Sunni Islam, Christianity
Currency: Lebanese Pound

Lesotho

A small, landlocked kingdom entirely surrounded by the Republic of SOUTH AFRICA. Snow-capped mountains and treeless uplands, cut by spectacular gorges, cover two-thirds of the country. The climate is pleasant with variable rainfall. Winters are generally dry with heavy frosts in lowland areas and frequent snow in the highlands. Because of the mountainous terrain, only one-eighth of the land can be cultivated and the main crop is maize. Yields are low because of soil erosion on the steep slopes and overgrazing by herds of sheep and cattle. Wool and mohair are exported but most foreign exchange comes from money sent home by Lesotho workers in South Africa.

Quick facts:
Area: 11,720 square miles (30,355 square
   kilometres)
Population: 2,022,000
Capital: Maseru
Form of government: Constitutional Monarchy
Religions: Christianity, traditional beliefs
Currency: Loti/South African Rand

Liberia

Located in West Africa, Liberia has a 348-mile (560-kilometres) coast stretching from Sierra Leone to Côte d'Ivoire. It is the only African country never to be ruled by a foreign power. It has a treacherous coast, with rocky cliffs and lagoons enclosed by sand bars. Inland the land rises to a densely forested plateau dissected by deep, narrow valleys. Farther inland still, there are beautiful waterfalls and the Nimba Mountains rise to a maximum height of 5,748 feet (1,752 metres). Agriculture employs three-quarters of the labour force and produces cassava and rice as subsistence crops and rubber, coffee and cocoa for export. Forest and animal reserves are magnificent and the beaches and lagoons are beautiful. The Nimba Mountains are rich in iron ore, which accounts for 70 per cent of export earnings and wood, rubber, diamonds and coffee are also exported. Liberia has a very large delivery tanker fleet, most of which have foreign owners. The economy has suffered greatly because of civil war, with food shortages and the drying up of foreign investment and the situation remains uncertain, leaving Liberia with considerable problems to overcome.

Quick facts:
Area: 43,000 square miles (111,369 square
  kilometres)
Population: 3,042,000
Capital: Monrovia
Other major city: Buchanan
Form of government: Republic
Religions: Traditional beliefs, Sunni Islam,
  Christianity
Currency: Liberian Dollar

Libya

A large North African country that stretches from the south coast of the Mediterranean to and in some parts beyond, the Tropic of Cancer. The Sahara covers much of the country, extending right to the Mediterranean coast at the Gulf of Sirte. The only green areas are the scrublands found in the northwest and the forested hills near Benghazi. The coastal area has mild wet winters and hot dry summers, but the interior has had some of the highest recorded temperatures of anywhere in the world. Around 18 per cent of the people work on the land, the main agricultural region being in the northwest, near Tripoli, but this is dependent on rainfall. The main crops produced are wheat, tomatoes, fruits and barley. Many sheep, goats and cattle are reared and there is an export trade in skins, hides and hairs. Libya is one of the world's largest producers of oil and natural gas and also produces potash and marine salt. Other industries include food processing, textiles, cement and handicrafts. The majority of consumer products are imported.

Quick facts:
Area: 679,362 square miles (1,759,540 square kilometres)
Population: 5,900,000
Capital: Tripoli (Tarabulus)
Other cities: Benghazi, Misrāta
Form of government: Socialist People's Republic
Religion: Sunni Islam
Currency: Libyan Dinar

Liechtenstein

The principality of Liechtenstein is a tiny central European state situated on the east bank of the River Rhine, bounded by Austria to the east and Switzerland to the west. To the east and south lie the foothills of the Austrian Alps. The highest peak, on the border with Switzerland, is Grauspitz at 8,527 feet (2,599 metres). The climate is mild alpine. Approximately one-third of the country is covered by forests and there are deer, fox, chamois and badger. Once an agricultural country, Liechtenstein has rapidly moved into industry in the last 30 years, with a variety of light industries such as textiles, high quality metal goods, precision instruments, ceramics and pharmaceuticals. It is a popular location for the headquarters of foreign companies in order that they can benefit from the favorable tax laws. Tourism also thrives, beautiful scenery and good skiing being the main attractions. Other income is derived from international banking and financial services and the sale of postage stamps.

Quick facts:
Area: 62 square miles (160 square kilometres)
Population: 33,987
Capital: Vaduz
Form of government: Constitutional Monarchy
  (Principality)
Religion: Roman Catholicism
Currency: Swiss Franc

Lithuania

A country that lies to the northwest of RUSSIA and BELARUS and is bounded to the north by LATVIA and west by POLAND. It is the largest of the three former Soviet Baltic republics. Before 1940 Lithuania was a mainly agricultural country but has since been considerably industrialised, with shipbuilding, food processing, petroleum refining and electrical machinery production being significant. Most of the land is lowland, covered by forest and swamp and the main agricultural products are rye, barley, sugar beet, flax, potatoes, meat, milk and fish. About 20 per cent of the population is engaged in agriculture, principally dairy farming and livestock production. Amber is found along the Baltic coast and used by Lithuanian craftsmen for making jewellery. The country's economy has improved dramatically since it became independent and joined the European Union in 2004.

Quick facts:
Area: 25,174 square miles (65,200 square
    kilometres)
Population: 3,585,300
Capital: Vilnius
Other cities: Kaunas, Klaipeda, Siauliai
Form of government: Parliamentary Democracy
Religion: Roman Catholicism
Currency: Litas

Luxembourg, Grand Duchy of

A small independent landlocked country bounded by BELGIUM on the west, FRANCE on the south and GERMANY on the east. In the north of the duchy a wooded plateau, the Oesling, rises to 1,804 feet (550 metres) and in the south a lowland area of valleys and ridges is known as the Gutland. Northern winters are cold and raw, with snow covering the ground for almost a month, but in the south winters are mild and summers cool. In the south the land is fertile and crops grown include maize, roots, tubers and potatoes, with livestock also being raised. It is in the south, also, that (declining) beds of iron ore are found and these form the basis of the country's iron and steel industry. The country is very industrialised, with the financial sector playing an increasingly important part in the country's economy, as is tourism. In the east, Luxembourg is bordered by the Moselle river in whose valley grapes are produced for wine. The capital, Luxembourg City, is the seat of the European Court of Justice.

Quick facts:
Area: 998 square miles (2,586 square kilometres)
Population: 474,400
Capital: Luxembourg City
Other cities: Esch-sur-Algette, Differdange, Dudelange
Form of government: Constitutional Monarchy (Duchy)
Religion: Roman Catholicism
Currency: Euro

Macau (Macao)

Formerly a Portuguese colony, Macao reverted to China in 1999, becoming a special administrative region under Chinese sovereignty. China has promised 50 years of non-interference in its economic and social systems. One of the most densely populated places in the world, Macao consists of a rocky, hilly peninsula, connected by a sandy isthmus to China's Zhongshan (Tangjiahuan) island and the two small islands of Taipa and Coloâne. A free port, it is a leading trade, fishing and tourist centre with gambling casinos and textile, clothing, toy, plastics, fireworks and food processing industries.

Quick facts:
Area: 7 square miles (18 square kilometres)
Population: 453,125
Capital: Macao
Form of government: Special Administrative
   Region of China
Religions: Buddhism, Roman Catholicism
Currency: Pataca

Macedonia, The Former Yugoslav Republic of (FYROM)

A country that, under the name of Macedonia, declared its independence from Yugoslavia in November 1991. However GREECE, angered at the use of 'Macedonia' – also the name of the neighbouring Greek province –imposed a trade embargo and convinced the United Nations not to recognise the nation's independence. In 1993, Macedonia was admitted to the UN after changing its official name to the Former Yugoslav Republic of Macedonia. In 1995 an agreement was reached with Greece whereby both countries would respect the territory, sovereignty and independence of the other, with Macedonia agreeing to adopt a new flag. A landlocked country, Macedonia shares its borders with ALBANIA, BULGARIA, Greece and Serbia and Montenegro. Its terrain is mountainous, covered by deep valleys, with several large lakes. The River Vardar is the country's longest river and divides the country, flowing into Greece and eventually emptying into the Aegean Sea. The climate consists of hot, dry summers and cold winters with considerable snow. It is the poorest of the six former Yugoslav republics but sustains itself through agriculture and the coal industries. Some of its natural resources include chromium, lead, zinc, nickel, iron ore and lumber. The country's stability has been badly affected by rebel fighting in the region but civil war has been avoided.

Quick facts:
Area: 9,928 square miles (25,713 square
    kilometres)
Population: 2,050,000
Capital: Skopje
Other cities: Kumanovo, Ohrid
Form of government: Republic
Religions: Eastern Orthodox, Islam
Currency: Macedonian Dinar

Madagascar

An island state situated off the southeast coast of Africa, separated from the mainland by the Mozambique Channel. Madagascar is the fourth largest island in the world and the centre of it is made up of high savanna-covered plateaus. In the east, forested mountains fall steeply to the coast and in the southwest the land falls gradually through dry grassland and scrub. The staple food crop is rice and although only 5 per cent of the land is cultivated, 80 per cent of the population grow enough to feed themselves. Cassava, potatoes, maize, beans and bananas are also grown, but some 58 per cent of the land is pasture and there are more cattle than people. The main export earners are coffee, vanilla, cloves and sugar cane. There is mining for chromite, graphite, mica and salt and an oil refinery at Toamasina on the east coast. Upon independence in 1960, Madagascar became known as the Malagasy Republic, but was changed back by referendum in 1975. Due to Madagascar's isolation from mainland Africa, there are several species of plants and animals that are quite different from mainland species. As a result, many tourists come to Madagascar to explore this aspect of the country's fauna and flora.

Quick facts:
Area: 226,658 square miles (587,041 square
  kilometres)
Population: 18,595,000
Capital: Antananarivo
Other cities: Fianarantsoa, Mahajanga,
  Toamasina, Toliara
Form of government: Republic
Religions: Traditional beliefs, Christianity, Islam
Currency: Madagascar Ariary

Malawi

A country that lies along the southern and western shores of the third largest lake in Africa, Lake Malawi. Malawi was formerly the British colony of Nyasaland, a name meaning 'Land of the Lake', which was given to it by the 19th-century explorer David Livingstone. To the south of the lake the Shire river flows through a valley overlooked by wooded, towering mountains. The tropical climate has a dry season from May to October and a wet season for the remaining months. Agriculture is the predominant occupation and many Malawians live off their own crops. Exports include tea grown on the terraced hillsides in the south and tobacco on the central plateau plus peanuts and sugar, with maize also being an important crop. Malawi has bauxite and coal deposits but because of the inaccessibility of their locations, mining is limited. Hydroelectricity is now being used for manufacturing but imports of manufactured goods remain high. The country remains one of the poorest in the world with political unrest and high rates of HIV infection contributing to its failing economy.

Quick facts:

Area: 45,747 square miles (118,484 square kilometres)

Population: 13,013,000

Capital: Lilongwe

Other cities: Blantyre, Zomba

Form of government: Republic

Religions: Traditional beliefs, Christianity, Islam

Currency: Malawian Kwacha

Malaysia

The Federation of Malaysia lies in the South China Sea in southeast Asia and comprises peninsular Malaysia on the Malay Peninsula and the states of Sabah and Sarawak on the island of Borneo. Malaysia is affected by the monsoon climate. The northeast monsoon brings rain to the east coast of peninsular Malaysia in winter and the southwest monsoon brings rain to the west coast in summer. Throughout the country the climate is generally tropical and temperatures are uniformly hot throughout the year. Peninsular Malaysia has always had thriving rubber-growing and tin-dredging industries and now oil palm-growing is also important on the east coast. Sabah and Sarawak have grown rich by exploiting their natural resources, the forests. There is also some offshore oil and around the capital, Kuala Lumpur, new industries such as electronics have expanded rapidly in recent years. Tourism has become an important industry. Malaysia was hit by economic recession in 1997 and implemented a series of measures designed to restore confidence in its economy which now remains healthy.

Quick facts:

Area: 127,320 square miles (329,758 square kilometres)
Population: 24,385,000
Capital: Kuala Lumpur
Other cities: Ipoh, George Town, Johor Baharu
Form of government: Federal Constitutional Monarchy
Religions: Islam, Buddhism, Hinduism, Christianity
Currency: Ringgit (Malaysian Dollar)

Maldives, Republic of

A country that lies 398 miles (640 kilometres) southwest of SRI LANKA in the Indian Ocean and comprises 1,200 low-lying coral islands grouped into 12 atolls. Roughly 202 of the islands are inhabited, and the highest point is only 5 feet (1.5 metres) above sea level. Independence was gained in 1965, with a republic being formed three years later. The climate is hot and humid and affected by monsoons from May to August. The islands are covered by coconut palms and some millet, cassava, yams and tropical fruit are grown. However, rice, the staple diet of its islanders, is imported. The most important natural resource is marine life and fishing is an important occupation. The chief export is now canned or frozen tuna. Tourism is now developing fast and has taken over from fishing as the major foreign currency earner.

Quick facts:
Area: 115 square miles (298 square
   kilometres)
Population: 359,000
Capital: Malé
Form of government: Republic
Religion: Sunni Islam
Currency: Rufiyaa

Mali

A landlocked state in West Africa, Mali is one of the world's poorest nations. The country mainly comprises vast and monotonous plains and plateaus. It rises to 3,790 feet (1,155 metres) in the Adrar des Iforas range in the northeast. The Sahara in the north of the country is encroaching southwards. In the south there is some rain and plains are covered by grassy savanna and a few scattered trees. The River Niger runs through the south of the country and small steamboats use it for shipping between Koulikoro and Gao. Fish are plentiful in the river and its water is used to irrigate the land. Only a fifth of the land can be cultivated. Rice, cassava and millet are grown for domestic consumption and cotton for export. Droughts in the 1970s and mid-1980s resulted in thousands of cattle dying and in crop failure, with famine and disease killing many of the population. The country's main exports include cotton, gold, foodstuffs, livestock and mangoes. Iron ore and bauxite have been discovered but have yet to be exploited.

Quick facts:

Area: 478,841 square miles (1,240,192 square
   kilometres)
Population: 11,716,000
Capital: Bamako
Other towns: Gao, Kayes, Ségou, Mopti,
   Sikasso
Form of government: Republic
Religions: Sunni Islam, traditional beliefs
Currency: CFA Franc

Malta

A small republic in the middle of the Mediterranean Sea, lying just south of the island of Sicily. It comprises three islands, Malta, Gozo and Comino, which are made up of low limestone plateaus with little surface water. The climate is Mediterranean, with hot, dry sunny summers and little rain. Lack of water has led to the production of desalination plants that produce up to 70 per cent of the country's needs. Winters are cooler and wetter. Malta has a long history of civilisation, with remains found from Stone and Bronze Age peoples. The country is virtually self-sufficient in agricultural products and exports potatoes, vegetables, wine and cut flowers. The British military base on Malta was once the mainstay of the economy but after the British withdrew in the late 1970s, a freight shipping industry and financial services industry helped transform the country's economy. Other industries include electronic and textile manufacturing. Tourism also boomed and the island has become popular for retirement in the sunshine with low taxes. Malta became a member of the European Union in 2004.

Quick facts:
Area: 122 square miles (316 square kilometres)
Population: 400,214
Capital: Valletta
Form of government: Republic
Religion: Roman Catholicism
Currency: Maltese Lira

Marshall Islands

Formerly part of the United States-administered United Nations territory, this self-governing republic comprises a scattering of over 1,000 coral atolls and islets, arranged in two parallel chains, Ratak and Ralik, located in eastern Micronesia in the western Pacific Ocean and lying to the northwest of KIRIBATI. The climate is tropical maritime, with little variation in temperature and rainfall that is heaviest from July to October. The republic remains in free association with the USA and the economy is almost totally dependent on US-related payments for use of the islands as bases. The Bikini Atoll was used as a nuclear testing area in 1946. The main occupations are fishing and agriculture, with the chief export being copra.

Quick facts:

Area: 70 square miles (181 square kilometres)
Population: 60,422
Capital: Dalag-Uliga-Darrit (on Majuro Atoll)
Form of government: Republic in free
  association with the USA
Religion: Christianity
Currency: US Dollar

Martinique

One of the larger of the islands in the Windward Islands group in the southern Caribbean, lying between Dominica and St Lucia. It is administered as a department of FRANCE. The centre of the island is mountainous, while the quality of its beaches has played a role in its development as a tourist resort. It has a volcano, Mont Pelée (4,750 feet /1,448 metres), that erupted in 1902, wiping out the town of St Pierre and killing all but one of its inhabitants. Martinique is periodically subjected to hurricanes that can cause considerable damage. The island's economy relies mainly on tourism with sugar, bananas, pineapples, citrus fruits, nutmeg and spices being grown in some parts of the island.

Quick facts:

Area: 425 square miles (1,102 square kilometres)
Population: 436,131
Capital: Fort-de-France
Form of government: Overseas Department of France
Religion: Roman Catholicism
Currency: Euro

Mauritania

A country nearly twice the size of France located on the west coast of Africa. About 47 per cent of the country is desert, the Sahara covering much of the north. The only settlements found in this area are around oases, where a little millet, dates and vegetables can be grown. The main agricultural regions are in the Senegal river valley in the south. The rest of the country is made up of the drought-stricken Sahel grasslands. The majority of the people are traditionally nomadic herdsmen, but severe droughts since the late 1960s and early 1970s killed about 70 per cent of the nation's animals and the population has settled along the Senegal river. As a result, vast shanty towns have sprung up around all the towns. Production of iron ore and other deposits provide the country's main exports but hopes for future prosperity have been pinned on newly discovered offshore reserves of oil and natural gas. Mauritania has also experienced some internal political unrest with a military coup taking place in 2005.

Quick facts:
Area: 395,956 square miles (1,025,520 square kilometres)
Population: 3,177,000
Capital: Nouakchott
Other cities: Kaédi, Nouadhibou
Form of government: Republic
Religion: Sunni Islam
Currency: Ouguiya

Mauritius

A beautiful island with tropical beaches, lying about 20 degrees south in the Indian Ocean, 497 miles (800 kilometres) east of MADAGASCAR and which gained independence in 1968. The islands of Rodrigues and Agalega are also part of Mauritius. Mauritius is a volcanic island with many craters surrounded by lava flows. The central plateau rises to over 2,625 feet (800 metres), then drops sharply to the south and west coasts. The climate is hot and humid, southwesterly winds bringing heavy rain in the uplands and there is the possibility of cyclones during December to April. The island has well-watered fertile soil, ideal for the sugar plantations that cover 45 per cent of the island. Although the export of molasses and sugar still dominate the economy, diversification is being encouraged. Other crops such as tea, tobacco, peanuts and vegetables are grown. The clothing and electronic equipment industries are becoming increasingly important and tourism is now the third largest source of foreign exchange.

Quick facts:

Area: 788 square miles (2,040 square kilometres)
Population: 1,240,000
Capital: Port Louis
Form of government: Republic
Religions: Hinduism, Roman Catholicism, Sunni Islam
Currency: Mauritian Rupee

Mexico

The most southerly country in North America. It has its longest border with the UNITED STATES to the north, a long coast on the Pacific Ocean and a smaller coast in the west of the Gulf of Mexico. It is a land of volcanic mountain ranges and high plateaus. The highest peak is Citlaltepetl, 18,697 feet (5,699 metres), which is permanently snow-capped. Coastal lowlands are found in the west and east. Its wide range of latitude and relief produce a variety of climates. In the north there are arid and semi-arid conditions while in the south there is a humid tropical climate. Thirty per cent of the labour force is involved in agriculture, growing maize, wheat, kidney beans and rice for subsistence and coffee, cotton, fruit and vegetables for export, although some irrigation is needed. Mexico has substantial and varied mineral deposits, such as silver, coal, phosphates, gold and uranium, as well as large reserves of oil and natural gas. Forests cover around a quarter of the country with trees such as ebony, mahogany and walnut. Developing industries are petrochemicals, textiles, motor vehicles and food processing. Tourism also makes an important contribution to the country's economy.

Quick facts:
Area: 756,066 square miles (1,958,201 square
  kilometres)
Population: 107,449,000
Capital: México City
Other cities: Guadalajara, León, Monterrey,
  Puebla, Tijuana
Form of government: Federal Republic
Religion: Roman Catholicism
Currency: Mexican Peso

Micronesia, Federated States of

Formerly part of the United States administered United Nations Trust Territory of the Pacific, known as the Caroline Islands, this self-governing republic became independent in 1990. It comprises an archipelago of over 600 islands, including Pohnpei (Ponape), Truk (Churk) Islands, Yap Islands and Kosrae. Mostly uninhabited, they are located in the western Pacific Ocean, about 2,500 miles (4,025 kilometres) southwest of Hawaii. The climate is tropical maritime, with high temperatures and rainfall all year round but a pronounced precipitation peak between July and October. Micronesia is still closely linked to the USA, with a heavy reliance on aid. Attempts are being made to diversify the economy, the exports of which are mainly fishing and copra. There are significant phosphate deposits but the island's isolation restricts development. Tourism is a growing trade but the economy of the region remains fragile.

Quick facts:
Area: 271 square miles (702 square kilometres)
Population: 108,000
Capital: Palikir
Form of government: Republic
Religion: Christianity
Currency: US Dollar

Moldova

A Soviet socialist republic from 1940 until 1991 when it became independent of the former USSR. It is bounded to the west by Romania and to the north, east and south by Ukraine. The republic consists of a hilly plain with an average height of around 500 feet (150 metres). Its main rivers are the Prut in the west and the Dnister in the north and east. Moldova's soils are fertile and crops grown include wheat, corn, barley, tobacco, sugar beet, soybeans and sunflowers. There are also extensive fruit orchards, vineyards and walnut groves. Wildlife is abundant, such as roe deer, weasels, martens and badgers. Beekeeping and silkworm breeding are widespread throughout the country. Food processing is the main industry, particularly sugar refining and wine making. Other industries include metal-working, engineering and the manufacture of electrical equipment. After independence, the economy declined and there has been ongoing unrest and conflict involving the region of Trans-Dniester which seeks independence from Moldova and a closer relationship with Russia.

Quick facts:

Area: 13,012 square miles (33,700 square
    kilometres)
Population: 4,466,000
Capital: Chisinau
Other cities: Tiraspol, Tighina, Bel'tsy
Form of government: Republic
Religion: Russian Orthodox
Currency: Moldovan Leu

Monaco

A tiny principality on the Mediterranean Sea, surrounded landwards by the Alpes Maritimes department of FRANCE. It comprises a rocky peninsula and a narrow stretch of coast. It has mild moist winters and hot dry summers. The ancient fortified town of Monaco is situated on a rocky promontory and houses the royal palace and the cathedral. The Monte Carlo district has its world-famous casino and La Condamine has thriving businesses, stores, banks and attractive residential areas. Fontvieille is an area reclaimed from the sea where marinas and light industry are now located. Light industry includes chemicals, plastics, electronics, engineering and paper, but it is tourism that is the main revenue earner. The sale of stamps, tobacco, insurance and banking industries also contribute to the economy. Well-known annual events such as the Monte Carlo Rally and Monaco Grand Prix are held in the principality.

Quick facts:
Area: 0.4 square mile (1 square kilometre)
Population: 32,000
Capital: Monaco
Form of government: Constitutional Monarchy
Religion: Roman Catholicism
Currency: Euro

Mongolia

A landlocked country in northeast Asia that is bounded to the north by RUSSIA and by CHINA to the south, west and east. Most of Mongolia is mountainous. In the northwest are the Hangayn Mountains and the Altai, rising to 14,312 feet (4,362 metres). In the south there are grass-covered steppes and the desert wastes of the Gobi. The climate is very extreme and dry, with long, very cold winters and short, mild summers. Agriculture, particularly the rearing of livestock, is the main economic activity and source of employment in Mongolia. Under Communism, all cultivation and livestock rearing was state-controlled but since 1990 Mongolia has moved towards a free market economy. Crops grown include cereals (wheat, barley and oats), potatoes and some other vegetables but cultivation is heavily dependent on irrigation. Mongolia has valuable reserves of iron ore, coal, copper, molybdenum, fluorspar, tungsten, uranium, gold and silver. Manufacturing industries are generally on a small scale and include the processing of wool, hides, leather, furs, meat and dairy produce, textiles, wooden goods, agricultural equipment and building products. The collapse of trade with the former USSR created economic problems for Mongolia. It now looks to Japan, the US and the European Union for trade and economic assistance but its main trading partners are still China and Russia.

Quick facts:

Area: 604,829 square miles (1,566,500 square kilometres)

Population: 2,832,000

Capital: Ulaanbaatar

Other cities: Altay, Saynshand, Hovd, Choybalsan, Tsetserleg

Form of government: Republic

Religions: Buddhism, Shamanism, Christianity, Islam

Currency: Togrok/Tughrik

Morocco

A country in northwest Africa strategically placed at the western entrance to the Mediterranean Sea. It is a land of great contrasts, with high rugged mountains, the arid Sahara And green Atlantic and Mediterranean coasts. The country is split from southwest to northeast by the Atlas Mountains. The north has a pleasant Mediterranean climate with hot dry summers and mild moist winters. Farther south winters are warmer and summers even hotter. Snow often falls in winter on the Atlas Mountains. Morocco is mainly a farming country, wheat, barley and maize being the main food crops and it is one of the world's chief exporters of citrus fruit although agriculture accounts for less than 20 per cent of the land use. Morocco's main wealth comes from phosphates, reserves of which are the largest in the world, while coal, lead, iron and manganese ores are also produced. Morocco is self-sufficient in textiles, has automobile assembly plants, soap and cement factories and a large sea fishing industry. Tourism is a major source of revenue. Recent economic policies have brought some stability to the country's economy but unemployment is high in urban areas and living standards for many are still very low.

Quick facts:

Area: 172,414 square miles (446,550 square kilometres)

Population: 33,241,000

Capital: Rabat

Other cities: Casablanca, Fès, Marrakech, Tangier

Form of government: Constitutional Monarchy

Religion: Sunni Islam

Currency: Moroccan Dirham

Mozambique

A republic located in southeast Africa and one of the world's poorest. A coastal plain covers most of the southern and central territory, giving way to the western highlands and north to a plateau including the Nyasa Highlands. The Zambezi river separates the high plateaus in the north from the lowlands in the south. The country has a humid tropical climate with highest temperatures and rainfall in the north. Normally conditions are reasonably good for agriculture but a drought in the early 1980s, followed a few years later by severe flooding, resulted in famine and more than 100,000 deaths. A lot of industry was abandoned when the Portuguese left the country and not taken over by the local people because of lack of expertise. The economy is now on the upturn although the subsequent costs of the civil war between 1977 and 1992, such as re-homing the many displaced persons, and the 2002 drought have had an adverse economic effect.

Quick facts:
Area: 309,496 square miles (799,380 square
    kilometres)
Population: 19,686,000
Capital: Maputo
Other towns: Beira, Nampula
Form of government: Republic
Religions: Traditional beliefs, Roman
    Catholicism, Sunni Islam
Currency: Metical

Myanmar, Union of (Burma)

Burma is the second largest country in Southeast Asia but also one of the poorest. It has been under military rule since 1962 and its economy is riddled with corruption. The heartland of the country is the valley of the Irrawaddy. The north and west of the country are mountainous and in the east the Shan Plateau runs along the border with THAILAND. The climate is equatorial at the coast, changing to tropical monsoon over most of the interior. The Irrawaddy river flows into the Andaman Sea, forming a huge delta area that is ideal land for rice cultivation. Rice is the country's staple food and accounts for half the country's export earnings. Tropical fruits such as bananas, mangoes, citrus and guavas grow well in the fertile coastal regions. Burma is rich in lumber and mineral resources such as natural gas, petroleum, jade and natural rubies, but because of poor communications, lack of development and ethnic unrest the resources have not been fully exploited which has at least contributed to the preservation of the country's natural environment.

Quick facts:
Area: 261,228 square miles (676,578 square kilometres)
Population: 47,382,000
Capital: Rangoon (Yangon)
Other cities: Mandalay, Moulmein, Pegu
Form of government: Republic
Religion: Buddhism
Currency: Kyat

Namibia

A country situated on the Atlantic coast of southwest Africa. There are three main regions in the country. Running down the entire Atlantic coastline is the Namib Desert, east of which is the Central Plateau of mountains, rugged outcrops, sandy valleys and poor grasslands. East again and north is the Kalahari Desert. Namibia has a poor rainfall, the highest falling at Windhoek, the capital. Even here it only amounts to 8–10 inches (200–250 millimetres) per year. It is essentially a stock-rearing country, with sheep, cattle and goats raised with subsistence agriculture mainly in the north. Diamonds are mined just north of the River Orange, as are other minerals such as silver, lead, uranium and copper. Namibia's output of diamonds amounts to almost a third of the world's total. One of Africa's richest fishing grounds lies off the coast of Namibia and mackerel, anchovies and pilchards are an important export although production has dropped in recent years because of overfishing.

Quick facts:

Area: 318,261 square miles (824,292 square
   kilometres)
Population: 2,044,000
Capital: Windhoek
Form of government: Republic
Religions: Christianity, traditional beliefs
Currency: Namibian Dollar/South African Rand

World Facts 144

Nauru

The world's smallest republic. It is an island situated just 25 miles (40 kilometres) south of the equator and is halfway between AUSTRALIA and Hawaii. It is an oval-shaped coral island only 12 miles (20 kilometres) in diametre and is surrounded by a reef. The centre of the island comprises a plateau that rises to 197 feet (60 metres) above sea level. Most of the population live along a narrow coastal belt of fertile land. The climate is tropical with a high and irregular rainfall. The country is rich, due entirely to the deposits of high quality phosphate rock in the central plateau. This is sold for fertiliser to Australia, NEW ZEALAND, JAPAN and KOREA. Phosphate deposits are likely to be exhausted in the near future but the government is investing overseas and attempting to diversify, with tourism and offshore banking being developed to help ensure the economic future of the country.

Quick facts:
Area: 8 square miles (21 square kilometres)
Population: 13,000
Capital: Nauru
Form of government: Republic
Religions: Protestantism, Roman Catholicism
Currency: Australian Dollar

Nepal, Kingdom of

A long narrow rectangular country, landlocked between CHINA and INDIA on the flanks of the eastern Himalayas. Its northern border runs along the mountain tops. In this border area is Mount Everest, at 29,028 feet (8,848 metres) the highest mountain in the world and Nepal also has the six other highest mountains within its borders. The climate is subtropical in the south and all regions are affected by the monsoon. Most of the population survive as peasant farmers. Some mineral deposits, such as copper, iron ore, mica and ochre, exist but, because of the country's inaccessible terrain, have not been completely charted. With Indian and Chinese aid, however, roads have been built from the north and south to Kathmandu. Nepal's main exports are carpets, foodstuffs, clothing and leather goods, with principal sources of foreign revenue being tourism and Gurkha soldiers' foreign earnings. Nepal now attracts thousands of visitors each year, many of whom belong to trekking and climbing expeditions, but unrest in the country has led to a decrease in tourism. Nepal is one of the world's poorest and least developed countries, a situation made worse by frequent changes of government and the ongoing struggle between government forces and Maoist rebels.

Quick facts:

Area: 56,827 square miles (147,181 square kilometres)
Population: 28,287,000
Capital: Kathmandu
Other city: Biratnagar
Form of government: Parliamentary Democracy and Constitutional Monarchy
Religions: Hinduism, Buddhism, Islam
Currency: Nepalese Rupee

Netherlands, The

Situated in northwest Europe, the Netherlands (also known as Holland) is bounded to the north and west by the North Sea. Around half of the Netherlands is below sea level and the Dutch have tackled some huge reclamation schemes to add some land area to the country. One such scheme is the Ijsselmeer, where four large reclaimed areas (polders) have added an extra 637 square miles (1,650 square kilometres) for cultivation and an overspill town for Amsterdam. The Netherlands has mild winters and cool summers. Natural vegetation is now confined mainly to grasses and heathers, with small areas of beech, ash, pine and oak forests being carefully maintained. Migratory birds visit the new habitats created by land reclamation. Agriculture and horticulture are highly mechanised and the most notable feature is the sea of glass under which salad vegetables, fruit and flowers are grown. Manufacturing industries include chemicals, machinery, petroleum, refining, metallurgy and electrical engineering. The main port of the Netherlands, Rotterdam, is the largest in the world.

Quick facts:
Area: 15,770 square miles (40,844 square
  kilometres)
Population: 16,491,000
Capital: Amsterdam
Seat of government: The Hague (s'Gravenhage)
Other cities: Rotterdam, Eindhoven
Form of government: Constitutional Monarchy
Religions: Roman Catholicism, Dutch Reformed,
  Calvinism
Currency: Euro

Netherlands Antilles

An autonomous country within the NETHERLANDS, spread over the southern Caribbean Sea and consisting of two sets of islands, the Southern Netherlands Antilles (Bonaire and Curaçao) and the Northern Netherlands Antilles (Saba, St Maarten and St Eustatius). The five islands are set to become individual territories in 2007, thus dissolving the federation: Curaçao and St Maarten will become autonomous territories of the Netherlands while Bonaire, St Eustatius and Saba will be given city status within the Netherlands. Saba is the highest island in the group rising to 2,854 feet (870 metres) at Mount Scenery. ARUBA was part of the group until 1986. The islands have a tropical climate. Oil refining and tourism are the most important economic activities.

Quick facts:
Area: 309 square miles (800 square kilometres)
Population: 221,736
Capital: Willemstad
Form of government: Autonomous Country
   within the Netherlands
Religion: Roman Catholicism
Currency: Netherlands Antillean Guilder

New Caledonia (Nouvelle Calédonie)

The most southerly of the Melanesian countries in the Pacific Ocean. It is a French Overseas Territory but there has been on-going unrest in the country between the indigenous Melanesian population and the French population over the question of independence. A 1998 Accord gave greater autonomy to the country and stipulated that an independence referendum should be held between 2014 and 2019. The main island, Nouvelle Calédonie, is 248 miles (400 kilometres) long and rises to a height of 5,377 feet (1,639 metres) at Mount Panie. The island is divided into two natural regions by the mountain range that runs down its centre: a dry west coast covered with gum tree savanna and a tropical east coast. It has a Mediterranean-type climate with rainfall at its heaviest between December and March. The country is rich in mineral resources, particularly nickel, which accounts for 90 per cent of its exports. Other exports include coffee and copra. The main tourist resorts are on the east coast of Nouvelle Calédonie.

Quick facts:
Area: 7,172 square miles (18,575 square
   kilometres)
Population: 219,246
Capital: Noumea
Form of government: French Overseas Territory
Religions: Roman Catholicism, Protestantism
Currency: CFP Franc

New Zealand

A country that lies southeast of AUSTRALIA in the South Pacific. It comprises two large islands (North Island and South Island), Stewart Island and the Chatham Islands and many smaller islands. The vast majority of the population live on North Island. New Zealand enjoys very mild winters with regular rainfall and no extremes of heat or cold. North Island is hilly, with isolated mountains, active volcanoes, hot mineral springs and geysers. Earthquakes occur, and in 1987 considerable damage was caused by one at Edgecumbe. On South Island, the Southern Alps run north to south, and the highest point is Mount Cook at 12,313 feet (3,753 metres). The Canterbury Plains lie to the east of the mountains. Two-thirds of New Zealand is suitable for agriculture and grazing. Meat, wool and dairy goods are the main products. Forestry supports the pulp and paper industry, and a considerable source of hydroelectric power produces cheap electricity for the manufacturing industry, which now accounts for 30 per cent of New Zealand's exports. Mining is also an important industry, with petroleum, natural gas, limestone, gold and iron ore being exploited.

Quick facts:

Area: 104,454 square miles (270,534 square kilometres)

Population: 4,076,000

Capital: Wellington

Other cities: Auckland, Christchurch, Dunedin, Hamilton

Form of government: Parliamentary Democracy

Religions: Anglicanism, Roman Catholicism, Presbyterianism

Currency: New Zealand Dollar

Nicaragua

A country that lies between the Pacific Ocean and the Caribbean Sea, on the isthmus of Central America, and is sandwiched between HONDURAS to the north and COSTA RICA to the south. The east coast contains forested lowland and is the wettest part of the country. Behind this is a range of volcanic mountains, and the west coast is a belt of savanna lowland running parallel to the Pacific coast. The western region, which contains the two huge lakes, Nicaragua and Managua, is where most of the population live. The whole country is subject to devastating earthquakes. Nicaragua is primarily an agricultural country and 65 per cent of the labour force work on the land. The main export crops are coffee, bananas, cotton, meat and gold. There are mineral deposits of gold, copper and silver, with gold being of prime importance, but the country's economy has been adversely affected by civil war and natural calamities such as Hurricane Mitch in 1998.

Quick facts:
Area: 50,193 square miles (130,668 square
kilometres)
Population: 4,663,000
Capital: Managua
Form of government: Republic
Religion: Roman Catholicism
Currency: Gold Cordoba

Niger

A landlocked republic in West Africa, just south of the Tropic of Cancer. Over half the country is covered by the encroaching Sahara in the north, and the south lies in the drought-stricken Sahel. In the extreme southwest corner, the River Niger flows through the country, and in the extreme southeast lies Lake Chad, but the rest of the country is very short of water. The people in the southwest fish and farm their own food, growing rice and vegetables on land flooded by the river. Farther from the river, crops have failed as a result of successive droughts. Niger is an agricultural country, mainly of subsistence farmers, with the raising of livestock being the major activity. It is looking to oil exploration and gold mining to boost its economy although uranium mined in the Aïr Mountains continues to be the country's largest foreign currency earner.

Quick facts:
Area: 489,191 square miles (1,267,000 square
    kilometres)
Population: 12,525,000
Capital: Niamey
Other cities: Agadez, Maradi, Tahoua, Zinder
Form of government: Republic
Religion: Sunni Islam
Currency: CFA Franc

Nigeria

A large and populous country in West Africa. From the Gulf of Guinea it extends north to the border with NIGER. It has a variable landscape, from the swampy coastal areas and tropical forest belts of the interior, to the mountains and savanna of the north. The two main rivers are the Niger and the Benue, and just north of their confluence lies the Jos Plateau. The climate is hot and humid, and rainfall, heavy at the coast, gradually decreases inland. The dry far north is affected by the Harmattan, a hot dry wind blowing from the Sahara. About three-quarters of the land is suitable for agriculture and a wide variety of crops is raised by the subsistence farmers, mainly on small, family-owned farms. The main agricultural products are cocoa, rubber, groundnuts and cotton, with only cocoa being of any export significance. The country depends on revenue from its crude petroleum exports, which have a low sulphur content and therefore produce less air pollution, making it attractive to American and European countries. Full independence was achieved by Nigeria in 1960 but due to several factors, including the complex ethnic make-up of the country, the country's progress has frequently been interrupted by strife and internal dissent.

Quick facts:
Area: 356,669 square miles (923,768 square
   kilometres)
Population: 131,859,000
Capital: Abuja
Other cities: Lagos, Onitsha, Enugu, Ibadan,
   Kano, Ogbomosho
Form of government: Federal Republic
Religions: Sunni Islam, Christianity, traditional
   beliefs
Currency: Naira

Northern Mariana Islands

The islands are situated in the northwest Pacific Ocean. In 1986, the islanders voted for commonwealth status in union with the USA and they were granted US citizenship. The country consists of mainly volcanic islands with coral limestone and lava shores. Tourism is the main industry.

Quick facts:

Area: 179 square miles (464 square kilometres)

Population: 82,450

Capital: Saipan

Form of government: Commonwealth in political union with the USA

Religions: Roman Catholicism, traditional beliefs

Currency: US Dollar

Norway

A country that occupies the western half of the Scandinavian peninsula in northern Europe and is surrounded to the north, west and south by water. It shares most of its eastern border with SWEDEN and almost one-third of the country is north of the Arctic Circle. It is a country of spectacular scenery, of fjords, cliffs, rugged uplands and forested valleys. It has some of the deepest fjords in the world and has a huge number of glacial lakes. The climate is temperate as a result of the warming effect of the Gulf Stream. Summers are mild and although the winters are long and cold, the waters off the west coast remain ice-free. The country's longest river is the Glåma. Some southern lakes are affected by acid rain, which concerns the country's environmentalists. Agriculture is chiefly concerned with dairying and fodder crops. Fishing is an important industry and the large reserves of forest, which cover just over a quarter of the country, provide lumber for export. Industry is now dominated by petrochemicals based on the reserves of Norwegian oil in the North Sea. There are almost 100 airports in the country and transport by water is still of importance.

Quick facts:
Area: 125,050 square miles (323,877 square kilometres)
Population: 4,610,000
Capital: Oslo
Other cities: Bergen, Trondheim, Stavanger, Kristiansand, Tromsö
Form of government: Constitutional Monarchy
Religion: Church of Norway
Currency: Norwegian Krone

Oman (the Sultanate of Oman)

Situated in the southeast of the Arabian Peninsula, Oman is a small country in two parts. It comprises a small mountainous area overlooking the Strait of Hormuz, which controls the entrance to The Gulf and the main part of the country, consisting of barren hills rising sharply behind a narrow coastal plain. Inland the hills extend into the unexplored Rub al Khali (The Empty Quarter) in Saudi Arabia. Oman has a desert climate with exceptionally hot and humid conditions from April to October and as a result of the extremely arid environment, less than one per cent of the country is cultivated, the main produce being dates and limes, which are exported. The economy is heavily dependent on oil, providing a large proportion of its exports, although there are deposits of asbestos, copper and marble. Tourism is another source of revenue. There are no political parties in Oman and the judicial system is centred on the law of Islam.

Quick facts:

Area: 119,498 square miles (309,500 square
  kilometres)
Population: 3,102,000
Capital: Mascat (Musqat)
Other towns: Salalah, Al Khaburah, Matrah
Form of government: Monarchy (Sultanate)
Religions: Ibadhi Islam, Sunni Islam, Shia Islam
Currency: Omani Rial

Pakistan (the Islamic Republic of Pakistan)

A country that lies just north of the Tropic of Cancer and has as its southern border the Arabian Sea. The valley of the Indus river splits the country into a highland region in the west and a lowland region in the east. A weak form of tropical monsoon climate occurs over most of the country and conditions in the north and west are arid. Earthquakes in the north and the west are frequent and often severe and flooding occurs along the Indus after heavy rains. Temperatures are high everywhere in summer but winters are cold in the mountains. Most agriculture is subsistence, with wheat and rice as the main crops. Cotton and rice are the main cash crops, but the cultivated area is restricted because of waterlogging and saline soils. Pakistan's wide range of mineral resources has not been extensively developed and industry concentrates on food processing, textiles, consumer goods and handicrafts, including carpets and pottery. Alternating periods of civilian and military rule together with ongoing regional conflicts have adversely affected the stability of the country.

Quick facts:

Area: 307,374 square miles (796,095 square kilometres)

Population: 165,803,000

Capital: Islamabad

Other cities: Faisalabad, Hyderabad, Karachi, Lahore, Rawalpindi

Form of government: Federal Islamic Republic

Religions: Sunni Islam, Shia Islam, Christianity, Hinduism

Currency: Pakistan Rupee

Palau

A republic consisting of a group of approximately 350 islands, lying in the western Pacific, 7 degrees north of the equator and about 625 miles (900 kilometres) equidistant from NEW GUINEA to the south and the PHILIPPINES to the west. A barrier reef to the west forms a large lagoon dotted with islands. Coral formations and marine life here are amongst the richest in the world. Formerly known as Belau, the republic has an agreement of free association with the United States. The main language is English. Subsistence fishing and agriculture are the mainstays of the economy but there is also some tourism. In addition, natural resources include minerals (particularly gold and sea-bed deposits) and forests.

Quick facts:
Area: 177 square miles (459 square
  kilometres)
Population: 20,579
Capital: Koror
Form of government: Republic in free
  association with the USA
Religions: Roman Catholicism, Modekngei
Currency: US Dollar

Panama

A country located at the narrowest point in Central America. Only 58 kilometres (36 miles) separates the Caribbean Sea from the Pacific Ocean at Panama, and the Panama Canal, which divides the country, is the main route from the Caribbean and the Atlantic to the Pacific. The climate is tropical, with high temperatures throughout the year and only a short dry season from January to April. The country is heavily forested and very little is cultivated. Rice is the staple food. The economy is heavily dependent on the Canal and income from it is a major foreign currency earner. The country has extensive lumber resources, and mahogany is an important export. Other exports include bananas, petroleum products, coffee, shrimps and raw sugar. In 1989 the country was briefly invaded by US military forces in order to depose the corrupt dictator General Noriega.

Quick facts:
Area: 29,157 square miles (75,517 square
     kilometres)
Population: 3,190,000
Capital: Panama City
Other cities: Colón, Puerto Armuelles, David
Form of government: Republic
Religion: Roman Catholicism
Currency: Balboa/US Dollar

Papua New Guinea

A country in the southwest Pacific, comprising the eastern half of the island of New Guinea together with hundreds of islands including New Britain, the Bismarck Archipelago and New Ireland. There are active volcanoes on some of the islands and mainland and almost 100,000 people were evacuated in 1994 when two erupted on New Britain. The country has a mountainous interior surrounded by broad swampy plains. The climate is tropical, with high temperatures and heavy rainfall. Subsistence farming is the main economic activity although some coffee, cocoa and copra are grown for cash. Lumber is cut for export and fishing and fish processing industries are developing. The country's wildlife is plentiful and varied, while the coastal waters support an abundance of sea life. Minerals such as copper, gold, silver and oil form the mainstay of the economy. The country still receives valuable aid from AUSTRALIA, which governed it before independence was gained in 1975.

Quick facts:

Area: 178,704 square miles (462,840 square
  kilometres)
Population: 5,670,000
Capital: Port Moresby
Form of government: Parliamentary
  Democracy
Religions: Protestantism, Roman Catholicism
Currency: Kina

Paraguay

A small landlocked country in central South America, bordered by BOLIVIA, BRAZIL and ARGENTINA. The climate is tropical, with abundant rain and a short dry season. The River Paraguay splits the country into the Chaco, a flat semi-arid plain on the west, and a partly forested undulating plateau on the east. Almost 95 per cent of the population live east of the river, where crops grown on the fertile plains include cassava, sugar cane, maize, cotton and soya beans. Immediately west of the river, on the low Chaco, are huge cattle ranches that provide meat for export. Although there are deposits of minerals such as iron, petroleum and manganese, these are not exploited commercially. The lumber industry is important, however, with tannin and petitgrain oil also being produced. With three important rivers, the Paraguay, Parana and Pilcomayo, the country has many impressive waterfalls, such as the Guaira Falls. In cooperation with its neighbours, it has developed its potential for hydroelectric power to the full and is able to meet all its energy needs. Years of political instability have, however, contributed to a lack of economic progress and some 60 per cent of the population live in poverty.

Quick facts:
Area: 157,048 square miles (406,752 square kilometres)
Population: 6,506,000
Capital: Asunción
Other cities: Concepción, Ciudad del Este, Encarnación
Form of government: Republic
Religion: Roman Catholicism
Currency: Guarani

Peru

A country located just south of the equator, on the Pacific coast of South America. It has three distinct regions from west to east: the coast, the high sierra of the Andes and the tropical jungle. The climate on the narrow coastal belt is mainly desert, while the Andes are wet and east of the mountains is equatorial with tropical forests. Most large-scale agriculture is in the oases and fertile, irrigated river valleys that cut across the coastal desert. Sugar and cotton are the main exports. Sheep, llamas, vicunas and alpacas are kept for wool. The fishing industry was once the largest in the world but recently the shoals have become depleted. Anchovies form the bulk of the catch and are used to make fish meal. Minerals such as iron ore, silver, copper and lead, as well as natural gas and petroleum, are extracted in large quantities and are an important part of the economy. The economy has been damaged by the declining value of exports, inflation, drought and guerrilla warfare and much of the population lives in poverty.

Quick facts:
Area: 496,225 square miles (1,285,216 square
  kilometres)
Population: 28,302,000
Capital: Lima
Other cities: Arequipa, Callao, Chiclayo,
  Cuzco, Trujillo
Form of government: Republic
Religion: Roman Catholicism
Currency: Nuevo Sol

Philippines

A country comprising a group of 7,107 islands and islets in the western Pacific that are scattered over a great area. There are four main groups: Luzon and Mindoro to the north, the Visayan Islands in the centre, Mindanao and the Sulu Archipelago in the south and Palawan in the southwest. Manila, the capital, is on Luzon. Most of the islands are mountainous and earthquakes are common. The climate is humid, with high temperatures and high rainfall. Typhoons can strike during the rainy season from July to October. Rice, cassava, sweet potatoes and maize are the main subsistence crops and coconuts, sugar cane, pineapples and bananas are grown. Agriculture employs around 42 per cent of the workforce. The mining industry produces gold, silver, nickel, copper and salt. Fishing is of some importance and other industries include textiles, food processing, chemicals and electrical engineering. The economy is largely dependent on the money sent home by the many Filipinos working overseas.

Quick facts:

Area: 115,813 square miles (300,000 square kilometres)

Population: 89,468,000

Capital: Manila

Other cities: Cebu, Davao, Quezon City, Zamboanga

Form of government: Republic

Religions: Sunni Islam, Roman Catholicism, Protestantism

Currency: Philippine Peso

Pitcairn Islands

A British overseas territory situated in the southeast Pacific Ocean. They are volcanic with high lava cliffs and rugged hills. The islanders are direct descendants of the HMS Bounty mutineers and their Tahitian wives. Subsistence agriculture produces a wide variety of tropical and subtropical crops but the sale of postage stamps is the country's main revenue earner.

Quick facts:

Area: 2 square miles (5 square kilometres)
Population: 50
Form of government: British Overseas
   Territory
Religion: Seventh Day Adventism
Currency: New Zealand Dollar

Poland

A country situated on the North European Plain. It borders GER-MANY to the west, the CZECH REPUBLIC and SLOVAKIA to the south and BELARUS and UKRAINE to the east. Poland consists mainly of lowlands and the climate is continental, marked by long severe winters and short warm summers. Over one-quarter of the labour force is involved in predominantly small-scale agriculture. The main crops are potatoes, wheat, barley, sugar beet and fodder crops. The industrial sector of the economy is large scale. Poland has large deposits of coal and reserves of natural gas, copper and silver and is a main producer of sulphur. Vast forests stretching inland from the coast supply the paper and furniture industries. Other industries include food processing, engineering, shipbuilding, textiles and chemicals. Poland became a member of the European Union in 2004 and the country has moved towards a market economy. Tourism has increased, with the Baltic resorts, mountains and cultural and historic sites being of prime importance.

Quick facts:
Area: 124,808 square miles (323,250 square kilometres)
Population: 38,536,000
Capital: Warsaw (Warszawa)
Other cities: Gdansk, Kraków, Lódz, Poznan, Wroclaw
Form of government: Republic
Religion: Roman Catholicism
Currency: Zloty

Portugal

A country in the southwest corner of Europe that makes up about 15 per cent of the Iberian Peninsula and is the least developed in western Europe. The most mountainous areas of Portugal lie to the north of the River Tagus. In the northeast are the steep-sided mountains of Tras-os-Montes and to south of this the Douro valley running from the Spanish border to Oporto on the Atlantic coast. South of the Tagus is the Alentajo, with its wheat fields and cork plantations, which continues to the hinterland of the Algarve with its beautiful groves of almond, fig and olive trees. Agriculture employs one-quarter of the labour force and crops include wheat, maize, grapes and tomatoes. Portugal's most important natural resources are its minerals, largely developed after World War II, including coal, iron ore, tin and copper. Port and Madeira wine are renowned and the country is a main exporter of olive oil. Manufacturing industry includes textiles, clothing, footwear, food processing and cork products. Tourism, particularly in the south, is the main foreign currency earner. A petrochemical plant and oil refinery is located near Lisbon and hydroelectric power has been developed in recent years. Portugal is also renowned for certain high quality craft products, especially lace, pottery and tiles.

Quick facts:

Area: 35,514 square miles (91,982 square
  kilometres)
Population: 10,605,800
Capital: Lisbon (Lisboa)
Other cities: Braga, Coimbra, Faro, Oporto,
  Setúbal
Form of government: Republic
Religion: Roman Catholicism
Currency: Euro

Puerto Rico

The most easterly of the Greater Antilles islands, lying in the Caribbean between the DOMINICAN REPUBLIC and the VIRGIN ISLANDS of the United States. It is a self-governing commonwealth in association with the USA and includes the main island, Puerto Rico, the two small islands of Vieques and Culebra and a fringe of smaller uninhabited islands. The climate is tropical, modified slightly by cooling sea breezes. The main mountains on Puerto Rico are the Cordillera Central, which reach 4,390 feet (1,338 metres) at the peak of Cerro de Punta. Dairy farming is the most important agricultural activity but the whole agricultural sector has been overtaken by industry in recent years. Tax relief and cheap labour encourage American businesses to be based in Puerto Rico. Products include textiles, clothing, electrical and electronic goods, plastics, pharmaceuticals and petrochemicals. Tourism is an important industry and there is potential for oil exploration both on and offshore. San Juan is one of the largest and best natural harbours in the Caribbean.

Quick facts:
Area: 3,427 square miles (8,875 square
  kilometres)
Population: 3,927,000
Capital: San Juan
Form of government: Self-governing
  commonwealth in association with the USA
Religions: Roman Catholicism, Protestantism
Currency: US Dollar

Qatar

A little emirate that lies halfway along the coast of The Gulf. It consists of a low barren peninsula and a few small islands. The climate is hot and uncomfortably humid in summer and the winters are mild with rain in the north. Most fresh water comes from natural springs and wells or from desalination plants. Some vegetables and fruit are grown but the herding of sheep, goats and some cattle is the main agricultural activity. The country is famous for its high quality camels. The discovery and exploitation of oil has resulted in a high standard of living for the people of Qatar, with some of the revenue being used to build hospitals and a road system and to provide free education and medical care. The Dukhan oil field has an expected life of 40 years and the reserves of natural gas are enormous. In order to diversify the economy, new industries such as iron and steel, cement, fertilisers and petrochemical plants have been developed.

Quick facts:

Area: 4,247 square miles (11,000 square
   kilometres)
Population: 885,000
Capital: Doha (Ad Dawhah)
Form of government: Monarchy (Emirate)
Religion: Wahhabi Sunni Islam
Currency: Qatari Riyal

Réunion

A French Overseas Department in the Indian Ocean, south of Mauritius. The island is mountainous and has one active and several extinct volcanoes. Most people live on the coastal lowlands and the economy is dependent upon tourism and the production of rum, sugar, maize, potatoes, tobacco and vanilla. French aid is given to the country in return for its use as a French military base.

Quick facts:
Area: 969 square miles (2,510 square
 kilometres)
Population: 787,000
Capital: St Denis
Form of government: French Overseas
 Department
Religion: Roman Catholicism
Currency: Euro

Romania

Apart from a small extension towards the Black Sea, Romania is almost a circular country. It is located in southeast Europe, bordered by UKRAINE, HUNGARY, Serbia and Montenegro, and BULGARIA. The Carpathian Mountains run through the north, east and centre of Romania and these are enclosed by a ring of rich agricultural plains that are flat in the south and west but hilly in the east. The core of Romania is Transylvania within the Carpathian arc. Romania's main river is the Danube, which forms a delta in its lower course. The country has cold snowy winters and hot summers. Agriculture in Romania has been neglected in favour of industry, but major crops include maize, sugar beet, wheat, potatoes and grapes for wine. Industry includes mining, metallurgy, mechanical engineering and chemicals. Forests support lumber and furniture-making industries in the Carpathians. After the overthrow of the Communist regime in 1989, a new constitution was approved by referendum. The post-communist government worked to bring about changes and improve the economy and Romania joined the European Union in 2007.

Quick facts:

Area: 92,043 square miles (238,391 square
  kilometres)
Population 22,303,000
Capital: Bucharest (Bucuresti)
Other cities: Brasov, Constanta, Galati, Iasi,
  Timisoara, Craiova, Brâila, Arad, Ploiesti
Form of government: Republic
Religions: Romanian Orthodox, Roman
  Catholicism
Currency: New Leu

Russia (the Russian Federation)

The largest country in the world (with over one-ninth of the world's land area) that extends from eastern Europe through the Ural Mountains east to the Pacific Ocean. The Caucasus Range forms its boundary with GEORGIA and AZERBAIJAN and it is here that the highest peak in Europe, Mt Elbrus (18,510 feet/5,642 metres), is located. In the east, Siberia is drained toward the Arctic Ocean by the great Rivers Ob, Yenisey and Lena and their tributaries. Just to the south of the Central Siberian Plateau lies Lake Baikal, the world's deepest freshwater lake (5,370 feet/1,637 metres). The Ural Mountains form the boundary between Asia and Europe and are where a variety of mineral resources are found. The environment ranges from vast frozen wastes in the north to subtropical deserts in the south. Agriculture is organised into either state or collective farms that mainly produce sugar beet, cotton, potatoes and vegetables. The country has extensive reserves of coal, oil, gas, iron ore and manganese. Major industries include the production of gas, iron and steel, cement, transport equipment, engineering, armaments. The Russian economy is recovering from a collapse in 1998 but the country is still beset by many problems including the ongoing conflict in Chechnya.

Quick facts:

Area: 6,592,850 square miles (17,075,400 square kilometres)

Population: 142,893,000

Capital: Moscow (Moskva)

Other cities: St Petersburg, Nizhniy Novgorod, Novosibirsk, Samara

Form of government: Republic

Religions: Russian Orthodox, Sunni Islam, Shia Islam, Roman Catholicism

Currency: Russian Ruble

Rwanda

A small republic in the heart of central Africa that lies just 2 degrees south of the equator. It is a mountainous country with a central spine of highlands from which streams flow west to the Congo river and east to the Nile. Active volcanoes are found in the north where the land rises to about 14,765 feet (4,500 metres). The climate is highland tropical, with temperatures decreasing with altitude. The soils are not fertile and subsistence agriculture dominates the economy. Staple food crops are sweet potatoes, cassava, dry beans, sorghum and potatoes. There are problems of soil erosion, overgrazing and droughts leading to famine, making the country very dependent on foreign aid. The main cash crops are arabic coffee, tea and pyrethrum. There are major reserves of natural gas under Lake Kivu in the west, but these are largely unexploited. The country is, however, faced with massive upheaval and disruption of economic life following the tragic tribal genocide wars in 1994, with ethnic division and rivalry between the Hutus and Tutsis continuing.

Quick facts:

Area: 10,169 square miles (26,338 square
  kilometres)
Population: 8,648,000
Capital: Kigali
Other major city: Butare
Form of government: Republic
Religions: Roman Catholicism, traditional
  beliefs, Protestantism, Islam
Currency: Rwandan Franc

St Kitts (St Christopher) and Nevis

The islands of St Christopher (popularly known as St Kitts) and Nevis lie in the Leeward group in the eastern Caribbean and in 1983 became a sovereign democratic federal state with the British monarch as head of state. St Kitts consists of three extinct volcanoes linked by a sandy isthmus to other volcanic remains in the south. The highest point on St Kitts is Mount Liamuiga, 4,314 feet (1,315 metres) and the islands have a tropical climate. Around most of St Kitts sugar cane is grown on the fertile soil covering the gentle slopes. Sugar is the chief export crop but market gardening and livestock are being expanded on the steeper slopes above the cane fields. Some vegetables, coconuts, fruits and cereals are grown. Industry includes sugar processing, brewing, distilling and bottling. St Kitts has a major tourist development at Frigate Bay. Nevis, 2 miles (3 kilometres) south, is an extinct volcano. Farming is declining and tourism is now the main source of income.

Quick facts:
Area: 101 square miles (261 square kilometres)
Population: 41,000
Capital: Basseterre
Other major city: Charlestown
Form of government: Parliamentary Democracy
Religions: Anglicanism, Methodism
Currency: East Caribbean Dollar

St Helena

A volcanic island in the south Atlantic Ocean which is a British Overseas Territory and an administrative centre for the islands of Tristan da Cunha to the south and Ascension Island to the north. Napoleon Bonaparte was exiled here by the British from 1815 until his death in 1821. The main exports are fish, lumber and handicrafts.

Quick facts:
Area: 47 square miles (122 square kilometres)
Population: 5,200
Capital: Jamestown
Form of government: British Overseas Territory
Religion: Anglicanism
Currency: St Helenian Pound

St Lucia

One of the Windward Islands in the eastern Caribbean. It lies to the south of MARTINIQUE and to the north of ST VINCENT. It was controlled alternately by the French and the British for some 200 years before becoming fully independent in 1979. St Lucia is an island of extinct volcanoes and the highest peak is 3,117 feet (950 metres). In the west are Les Pitons, two green peaks that rise directly from the sea to over 2,460 feet (750 metres). The climate is tropical, with a rainy season from May to August. The economy depends on the production of bananas and, to a lesser extent, coconuts and mangoes. Production, however, is often affected by hurricanes, drought and disease. There is some manufacturing industry, which produces clothing, cardboard boxes, plastics, electrical parts and drinks and the country has two airports. Tourism is increasing in importance and Castries, the capital, is a popular calling point for cruise liners.

Quick facts:
Area: 240 square miles (622 square kilometres)
Population: 168,000
Capital: Castries
Form of government: Parliamentary Democracy
Religion: Christianity
Currency: East Caribbean Dollar

St Pierre and Miquelon

Two islands to the south of Newfoundland, Canada, which form
a self-governing territorial collectivity of FRANCE. They are the last
French possessions in North America and have a substantial fishing industry.

Quick facts:
Area: 93 square miles (240 square kilometres)
Population: 7,026
Capital: Saint Pierre
Form of government: French Overseas Territory
Religion: Roman Catholicism
Currency: Euro

St Vincent and the Grenadines

An island of the Lesser Antilles, situated in the eastern Caribbean between St Lucia and Grenada. It is separated from Grenada by a chain of some 600 small islands known as the Grenadines, the northern islands of which form the other part of the country. The largest of these islands are Bequia, Mustique, Canouan, Mayreau and Union. The climate is tropical, with very heavy rain in the mountains. St Vincent Island is mountainous and a chain of volcanoes runs up the middle of the island. The volcano Soufrière (4,049 feet/1,234 metres) is active and last erupted in 1979. Farming is the main occupation on the island. Bananas are an important export and it is the world's leading producer of arrowroot starch. There is little manufacturing and the government is trying to promote tourism. Unemployment is high, however and tropical storms are always a threat to crops.

Quick facts:
Area: 150 square miles (388 square kilometres)
Population: 117,000
Capital: Kingstown
Form of government: Parliamentary Democracy
Religion: Christianity
Currency: East Caribbean Dollar

Samoa (Western)

Called Western Samoa until 1997, a state that lies in the Polynesian sector of the Pacific Ocean, about 447 miles (720 kilometres) northeast of Fiji. It consists of seven small islands and two larger volcanic islands, Savai'i and Upolu. Savai'i is largely covered by volcanic peaks and lava plateaus. Upolu is home to two-thirds of the population and the capital, Apia. The climate is tropical, with high temperatures and very heavy rainfall. The islands have been fought over by the Dutch, British, Germans and Americans, but they now have the traditional Polynesians lifestyle. Subsistence agriculture is the main activity and copra, cocoa and coconuts are the main exports. Many tourists visit the grave of the Scottish writer Robert Louis Stevenson, who died here and whose home is now the official home of the king. There are some light manufacturing industries, including clothing manufacture and an automobile components' factory, which is now the largest private employer and major export industry.

Quick facts:
Area: 1,093 square miles (2,831 square
   kilometres)
Population: 176,000
Capital: Apia
Form of government: Constitutional Monarchy
Religion: Christianity
Currency: Tala

Samoa, American

An unincorporated territory of the USA, lying close to Samoa in the Pacific Ocean and comprising five main volcanic islands and two coral atolls. The bulk of the population live on the islands of Tutaila and Ta'u. The five main islands are hilly and for the most part covered in thick forest or bush and the climate is tropical with lots of rain. The chief exports are canned tuna, pet foods, watches and handicrafts.

Quick facts:

Area: 77 square miles (199 square kilometres)

Population: 57,000

Capital: Pago Pago

Form of government: Unincorporated territory of the USA

Religion: Christianity

Currency: US Dollar

San Marino

A tiny landlocked state in central ITALY, lying in the eastern foothills of the Apennines and one of the smallest republics in the world. Tradition has it that in AD 301, a Christian sought refuge from persecution on Mount Titano. The resulting community prospered and was recognised in 1291 by Pope Nicholas IV as being independent. San Marino has wooded mountains and pasture land clustered around Mount Titano's limestone peaks, which rise to 2,425 feet (739 metres). San Marino has a mild Mediterranean climate. Most of the population work on the land or in forestry. Wheat, barley, maize, olives and vines are grown and the main exports are wood machinery, chemicals, wine, textiles, tiles, varnishes and ceramics, while dairy produce is the main agricultural product. Some 3.5 million tourists visit the country each year and much of the country's revenue comes from the sale of stamps, postcards, souvenirs and duty-free liquor. Italian currency is in general use but San Marino issues its own coins. In 1992 San Marino became a member of the United Nations and it is a full member of the Council of Europe.

Quick facts:

Area: 24 square miles (61 square kilometres)
Population: 29,000
Capital: San Marino
Other cities: Borgo Maggiore, Serravalle
Form of government: Republic
Religion: Roman Catholicism
Currency: Euro

São Tomé and Príncipe

A state comprising two volcanic islands that lie off the west coast of Africa. São Tomé is covered in extinct volcanic cones, reaching 6,641 feet (2,024 metres) at the highest peak. The coastal areas are hot and humid. Príncipe is a craggy island lying to the northeast of São Tomé. The climate is tropical, with heavy rainfall from October to May. Seventy per cent of the workforce work on the land, mainly in state-owned cocoa plantations that were nationalised in 1975, after independence. The other main agricultural products are coconuts, melons, copra, bananas and melons. Since crops grown are primarily for export, about 90 per cent of food has to be imported. Small manufacturing industries include food processing and lumber products. The islands were colonised by the Portuguese in the 15th century. They settled convicts and other exiles on the islands, developed a slave trade and grew sugar cane.

Quick facts:
Area: 372 square miles (964 square kilometres)
Population: 193,000
Capital: São Tomé
Form of government: Republic
Religion: Roman Catholicism
Currency: Dobra

Saudi Arabia

A state that occupies over 70 per cent of the Arabian Peninsula. Over 95 per cent of the country is desert and the largest expanse of sand in the world, Rub al Khali (the Empty Quarter), is found in the southeast of the country. In the west, a narrow, humid coastal plain along the Red Sea is backed by steep mountains. The climate is hot, with very little rain and some areas have no precipitation for years. The government has spent a considerable amount on reclamation of the desert for agriculture and the main products are dates, tomatoes, watermelons and wheat, which are grown in the fertile land around the oases. Saudi Arabia exports wheat and shrimps and is self-sufficient in some dairy products. The country's prosperity, however, is based almost entirely on the exploitation of its vast reserves of oil and natural gas. Industries include petroleum refining, petrochemicals and fertilisers. Saudi Arabia is one of the most important countries in the Arab and Muslim world because it is the place where Islam was born and because it is one of the world's biggest oil producers.

Quick facts:
Area: 830,000 square miles (2,149,690 square
  kilometres)
Population: 27,019,000
Capital: Riyadh (Ar Riyād)
Other cities: Ad Dammam, Mecca, Jeddah,
  Medina
Form of government: Monarchy
Religions: Wahhabi Islam, Sunni Islam, Shia
  Islam
Currency: Saudi Riyal

Senegal

A former French colony in West Africa that extends from the most western point in Africa, Cape Verde, to the border with MALI. Senegal is mostly low-lying and covered by savanna. The Fouta Djallon Mountains in the south rise to 4,971 feet (1,515 metres). The climate is tropical, with a dry season from October to June. The most densely populated region is in the southwest. Almost 80 per cent of the labour force work in agriculture, growing peanuts and cotton for export and millet, sugar cane, maize, rice and sorghum as subsistence crops. Increased production of crops such as rice and tomatoes is encouraged in order to achieve self-sufficiency in food. The country's economy is largely dependent on peanuts but there is a growing manufacturing sector, including food processing, cement, chemicals and tinned tuna. Money sent home by Senegalese working abroad is also important to the economy as is an expanding tourism industry but Senegal is still dependent on foreign aid. Its troops have often played an international peacekeeping role.

Quick facts:
Area: 75,955 square miles (196,722 square kilometres)
Population: 8,572,000
Capital: Dakar
Other cities: Kaolack, Thiès, St Louis
Form of government: Republic
Religions: Sunni Islam, Roman Catholicism
Currency: CFA Franc

Serbia and Montenegro (Union of)

The Union of Serbia and Montenegro is a remnant of the former Yugoslavia whose six constituent republics were Serbia, CROATIA, SLOVENIA, BOSNIA-HERZEGOVINA, MACEDONIA and Montenegro. The union will soon no longer exist as both Serbia and Montenegro have declared their independence after a referendum in Montenegro in 2006 when 55% of the population voted for separation from Serbia. Thus Serbia and Montenegro will soon be two separate and sovereign republics. The future status of Kosovo – an autonomous province of Serbia which remains an international protectorate but is still legally part of Serbia – is undecided and the subject of UN-sponsored talks. The terrain is very varied from rich fertile plains in the north to rugged mountains and hills in the south. The coastline of Montenegro is highly indented. Agriculture is one of the main industries and produce includes wheat, maize, grapes and citrus fruit. Forestry is also an important industry. Serbia contains important mineral reserves, with copper, antimony, lead, bauxite, coal, petroleum, natural gas, zinc, chromium and gold all being present. Other economic activities include mining and the manuafacture of iron and steel, chemicals, machinery, electronic equipment, textiles and clothing.

Quick facts:
Area: 39,449 square miles (102,173 square kilometres)
Population: 10,574,000
Capital: Belgrade (Beograd)
Other cities: Nis, Novi Sad, Pristina
Form of government: (Union of) Republics
Religions: Eastern Orthodox, Islam, Christianity
Currency: New Yugoslav Dinar (Serbia)/Euro (Montenegro)

Seychelles

A group of volcanic islands that lie in the western Indian Ocean, about 746 miles (1,200 kilometres) from the coast of East Africa. About 40 of the islands are mountainous and consist of granite while just over 50 are coral islands. The climate is tropical maritime with heavy rain. About 90 per cent of the people live on the island of Mahé, which is the site of the capital, Victoria. The staple foods are coconut, imported rice and fish, while some fruits are grown for home consumption Tourism accounts for about 90 per cent of the country's foreign exchange earnings and employs one-third of the labour force. Export trade is based on fish, petroleum (after importation), copra and cinnamon bark. The only mineral resource is guano. The Seychelles were a one-party socialist state until 1991, when a new constitution was introduced. The first free elections were held in 1993 and the country now enjoys stability and prosperity.

Quick facts:
Area: 175 square miles (455 square kilometres)
Population: 81,500
Capital: Victoria
Form of government: Republic
Religion: Roman Catholicism
Currency: Seychelles Rupee

Sierra Leone

A country on the Atlantic coast of West Africa, bounded by GUINEA to the north and east and by LIBERIA to the southeast. The country possesses a fine natural harbour where the capital and major port of Freetown is situated. A range of mountains, the Sierra Lyoa, rise above the capital on the Freetown Peninsula but, elsewhere, the coastal plain is up to 70 miles (110 kilometres) wide rising to a plateau and then mountains which are part of the Guinea Highlands Massif. The climate is tropical, with heavy rain during a rainy season lasting from May to November. The main food of the population is rice that is grown in the swamplands at the coast by the subsistence farmers. Other crops raised include sorghum, cassava, millet, sugar and peanuts. In the tropical forest areas, small plantations produce coffee, cocoa and palm oil. In the plateau much forest has been cleared for the growing of groundnuts. Most of the country's revenue comes from agriculture and mining, principally of rutile, although bauxite is produced in significant quantities. Diamonds are also mined and there are deposits of iron ore with some gold and platinum. Problems arising from a decade of civil war that ended in 2003 include poverty and tribal rivalry. Reconstruction is being aided by the export of diamonds and the exploitation of the country's mineral reserves.

Quick facts:

Area: 27,699 square miles (71,740 square
    kilometres)
Population: 6,005,000
Capital: Freetown
Other city: Bo
Form of government: Republic
Religions: Traditional beliefs, Sunni Islam,
    Christianity
Currency: Leone

Singapore

One of the world's smallest yet most successful countries. The city-state comprises one main island and 58 islets that are located at the foot of the Malay Peninsula in Southeast Asia. The main island of Singapore is very low-lying and the climate is hot and wet throughout the year. Only 1.6 per cent of the land area is used for agriculture, most food being imported. The country has a flourishing manufacturing industry for which it relies heavily on imports. Products traded in Singapore include machinery and electronic appliances, petroleum, food and beverages, chemicals, transport equipment, paper products and printing and clothes. The financial services industry is an important contributor to the country's economy and tourism is an important source of foreign revenue. The country's population enjoy one of highest standards of living in the world.

Quick facts:
Area: 239 square miles (618 square
    kilometres)
Population: 4,492,000
Capital: Singapore
Form of government: Parliamentary Republic
Religions: Buddhism, Sunni Islam, Christianity,
    Hinduism
Currency: Singapore Dollar

Slovakia (Slovak Republic)

A country that was constituted on 1 January 1993 as a new independent nation, following the dissolution of the 74-year-old federal republic of Czechoslovakia. Landlocked in central Europe, its neighbours are the CZECH REPUBLIC to the west, POLAND to the north, AUSTRIA and HUNGARY to the south and a short border with UKRAINE in the east. The northern half of the republic is occupied by the Tatra Mountains, which form the northern arm of the Carpathian Mountains. This region has vast forests and pastures used for intensive sheep grazing and is rich in high-grade minerals such as copper, iron, zinc and lead. The southern part of Slovakia is a plain drained by the Danube and its tributaries. Farms, vineyards, orchards and pastures for stock form the basis of southern Slovakia's economy. Slovakia has many economic and environmental problems as a legacy of the inefficient industrialisation of the old regime. In the early 1990s unemployment increased and inflation was high, resulting in a lowering in the standard of living but more recent economic reforms have seen an increase in foreign investment. Slovakia became a member of the European Union in 2004.

Quick facts:

Area: 18,928 square miles (49,035 square
  kilometres)
Population: 5,374,000
Capital: Bratislava
Other cities: Kosice, Zilina, Nitra
Form of government: Parliamentary Democracy
Religion: Roman Catholicism
Currency: Slovak Koruna

Slovenia

A republic that made a unilateral declaration of independence from former Yugoslavia on 25 June 1991. Sovereignty was not formally recognised by the European Community and the United Nations until early in 1992. It is bounded to the north by AUSTRIA, to the west by ITALY, to the east by HUNGARY and to the south by CROATIA. Most of Slovenia is situated in the Karst Plateau and in the Julian Alps, which has Mount Triglav as its highest point at 9,393 feet (2,863 metres). The Julian Alps are renowned for their scenery and the Karst Plateau contains spectacular cave systems. Although farming and livestock raising are the chief occupations, Slovenia is very industrialised and urbanised. Iron, steel and aluminium are produced and mineral resources include oil, coal, lead, uranium and mercury. There is also natural gas and petroleum. Slovenia has also been successful in establishing many new light industries, and this has given the country a well-balanced economic base for the future, with unemployment lessening and industrial output increasing. The northeast of the republic is famous for its wine production and tourism is also an important industry. Slovenia became a member of the European Union in 2004.

Quick facts:
Area: 7,821 square miles (20,256 square kilometres)
Population: 2,010,000
Capital: Ljubljana
Other cities: Maribor, Kranj
Form of government: Republic
Religion: Roman Catholicism, Orthodox, Islam
Currency: Tolar

Solomon Islands

A state that lies in an area between 5 and 12 degrees south of the equator, to the east of PAPUA NEW GUINEA, in the Pacific Ocean. The nation consists of six large islands and innumerable smaller ones. The larger islands are mountainous and covered by forests, with rivers prone to flooding. Guadalcanal is the main island and the site of the capital, Honiara. The climate is hot and wet and typhoons are frequent. The main food crops grown are coconut, cassava, sweet potatoes, plantains, yams, rice, taros and bananas. Other products include copra, processed fish, lumber and trochus shells. Mineral resources such as phosphate rock and bauxite are found in large amounts and some alluvial gold is produced. Other industries include palm oil-milling, sawmilling, food, tobacco and sodas. There are high rates of unemployment and illiteracy among the people and civil conflict has brought the country close to anarchy. An Australian peacekeeping force that arrived in the country in 2003 aims to restore order and stability in the country.

Quick facts:
Area: 11,157 square miles (28,896 square kilometres)
Population: 552,000
Capital: Honiara
Form of government: Parliamentary Democracy
Religion: Christianity
Currency: Solomon Islands Dollar

Somalia

A country that lies on the horn of Africa's east coast. It is bounded on the north by the Gulf of Aden and on the south and east by the Indian Ocean, and its neighbours include DJIBOUTI, ETHIOPIA and KENYA. The country is arid and most of it is low plateau with scrub vegetation. Its two main rivers, the Juba and Shebelle, are used to irrigate crops. Most of the population live in the mountains and river valleys and there are a few towns on the coast. The country has little in the way of natural resources but there are deposits of copper, petroleum, iron, manganese and marble, although not commercially exploited. Main exports are live animals, meat, hides and skins. A few large-scale banana plantations are found by the rivers. Years of drought have left Somalia heavily dependent on foreign aid and many of the younger people are emigrating to oil-rich Arab states. Civil war in the 1980s and early 1990s resulted in a huge loss of life and widespread famine. International UN peacekeeping forces were deployed and humanitarian aid given to try to avert a catastrophe but the forces withdrew in 1995. The situation remains unresolved although there has been some recovery in agriculture and food production.

Quick facts:

Area: 246,201 square miles (637,657 square
   kilometres)
Population: 9,822,000
Capital: Mogadishu (Muqdisho)
Other major towns: Hargeysa, Burco
Form of government: Republic
Religion: Sunni Islam
Currency: Somali Shilling

South Africa

A republic that lies at the southern tip of the African continent with a huge coastline on both the Atlantic and Indian Oceans. It occupies a huge saucer-shaped plateau, surrounding a belt of land that drops in steps to the sea. The rim of the saucer rises in the east to 11,424 feet (3,482 metres) in the Drakensberg Mountains. In general the climate has plenty of sunshine and relatively low rainfall. This varies with latitude, distance from the sea and altitude. Of the total land area, 58 per cent is used as natural pasture although soil erosion is a problem. The main crops grown are maize, sorghum, wheat, groundnuts, cotton and sugar cane. South Africa has great mineral wealth including gold, coal, copper, iron ore, manganese, diamonds and chrome ore. A system of apartheid existed in South Africa from 1948 until the early 1990s, denying black South Africans civil rights and promoting racial segregation. In 1990 F. W. de Klerk, then president, lifted the ban on the outlawed African National Congress and released its leader, Nelson Mandela. This heralded the dismantling of the apartheid regime and in the first multiracial elections, held in 1994, the ANC triumphed, with Mandela voted in as the country's president. Since that time South Africa has once again become an active and recognised member of the international community.

Quick facts:

Area: 471,445 square miles (1,221,037 square kilometres)

Population: 44,187,000

Capital: Pretoria (administrative), Cape Town (legislative)

Other cities: Johannesburg, Durban, Port Elizabeth, Soweto

Form of government: Republic

Religions: Christianity, Hinduism, Islam

Currency: Rand

Spain

A country located in southwest Europe and occupying the greater part of the Iberian Peninsula, which it shares with PORTUGAL. It is a mountainous country, sealed off from the rest of Europe by the Pyrénées, which rise to over 11,155 feet (3,400 metres). Much of the country is a vast plateau, the Meseta Central, cut across by valleys and gorges. Its longest shoreline is the one that borders the Mediterranean Sea. Most of the country has a form of Mediterranean climate, with mild moist winters and hot dry summers. Spain's major rivers, such as the Douro, Tagus and Guadiana, flow to the Atlantic Ocean while the Guadalquivir is the deepest. Although not generally navigable, they are of use for hydroelectric power. Spain's principal agricultural products are cereals, vegetables and potatoes and large areas are under vines for the wine industry. The soil is good, with almost one-third cultivable. Livestock production is important, particularly sheep and goats. Industry represents 72 per cent of the country's export value and production includes textiles, paper, cement, steel and chemicals. Tourism is a major revenue earner, especially from the resorts on the east coast.

Quick facts:
Area: 195,365 square miles (505,992 square kilometres)
Population: 40,397,000
Capital: Madrid
Other cities: Barcelona, Valencia, Seville, Zaragoza, Malaga, Bilbao
Form of government: Constitutional Monarchy
Religion: Roman Catholicism
Currency: Euro

Sri Lanka

A teardrop-shaped island in the Indian Ocean, lying south of the Indian Peninsula, from which it is separated by the Palk Strait. The climate is equatorial, with a low annual temperature range, but it is affected by both the northeast and southwest monsoons. Rainfall is heaviest in the southwest while the north and east are relatively dry. Agriculture engages 47 per cent of the work force and the main crops are rice, tea, rubber and coconuts, although sugar, rice and wheat have to be imported. Amongst the chief minerals mined and exported are precious and semiprecious stones. Graphite is also important. The main industries are food, beverages, tobacco, textiles, clothing, leather goods, chemicals and plastics. Politically, Sri Lanka has been afflicted by ethnic divisions between the Sinhalese and Tamils and civil war over a period of nearly two decades has damaged the economy of the country. The situation remains extremely volatile. The tourism industry in particular has been adversely affected and it was also badly hit by the Asian tsunami of 2004 which devastated much of the country's shoreline.

Quick facts:

Area: 25,332 square miles (65,610 square kilometres)
Population: 20,222,000
Capital: Colombo
Other cities: Trincomalee, Jaffna, Kandy, Moratuwa
Form of government: Republic
Religions: Buddhism, Hinduism, Christianity, Sunni Islam
Currency: Sri Lankan Rupee

Sudan

The largest country in Africa, lying just south of the Tropic of Cancer in northeast Africa. The country covers much of the upper Nile basin and in the north the river winds through the Nubian and Libyan deserts, forming a palm-fringed strip of habitable land. The climate is tropical and temperatures are high throughout the year. In winter, nights are very cold. Rainfall increases in amount from north to south, the northern areas being virtually desert. Sudan is an agricultural country, subsistence farming accounting for 80 per cent of production and livestock are also raised. Cotton is farmed commercially and accounts for about two-thirds of Sudan's exports. Gold is mined and there are large oil reserves. Sudan is the world's greatest source of gum arabic, used in medicines, perfumes, processed foods and inks. Other forest products are tannin, beeswax, senna and lumber. Because of a combination of years of civil war – between the mainly Muslim north and the Christian and Animist south – and drought, Sudan's infrastructure is badly damaged and the country is in need of reconstruction. Fighting in the Darfur region has led to a humanitarian crisis.

Quick facts:

Area: 967,500 square miles (2,505,813 square kilometres)
Population: 41,236,000
Capital: Khartoum (El Khartum)
Other cities: Omdurman, Khartoum North, Port Sudan
Form of government: Republic
Religions: Sunni Islam, traditional beliefs, Christianity
Currency: Sudanese Dinar

Surinam

A republic in northeast South America that was formerly known as Dutch Guiana. It is bordered to the west by GUYANA, to the east by GUIANA and to the south by BRAZIL. The country, formerly a Dutch colony, declared independence in 1975. It is one of the most ethnically diverse countries in the world. Suriname comprises a swampy coastal plain, a forested central plateau and southern mountains. The climate is tropical, with heavy rainfall concentrated mainly from December to April. Agriculture remains fairly underdeveloped. Crops cultivated include rice, bananas, citrus fruits, sugar cane, coffee and cocoa. Molasses and rum are produced along with some manufactured goods and there is an important coastal shrimp fishery. Suriname's economy is based on the mining of bauxite, which accounts for 80 per cent of its exports. The country has important mineral reserves of iron ore, nickel, copper, platinum and gold. Suriname's natural resources also include oil and lumber and forestry is an expanding industry. However, the country is politically unstable and faces many economic problems.

Quick facts:

Area: 63,037 square miles (163,265 square kilometres)
Population: 439,000
Capital: Paramaribo
Form of government: Republic
Religions: Hinduism, Roman Catholicism, Sunni Islam, traditional beliefs
Currency: Surinam Dollar

Swaziland

A landlocked hilly enclave almost entirely within the borders of the Republic of SOUTH AFRICA, Swaziland is an absolute monarchy. The mountains in the west of the country rise to about 6,500 feet (almost 2,000 metres), then descend in steps of savanna towards hilly country in the east. The climate is subtropical, moderated by altitude. The land between 1,300–2,800 feet (approximately 400–850 metres) is planted with orange groves and pineapple fields, while on the lower land sugar cane flourishes in irrigated areas. Lost trading concessions mean many in the sugar industry have recently lost their jobs. Forestry production centres mainly on pine since it matures extremely quickly because of Swaziland's climate. Coal is mined and manufacturing includes fertilisers, textiles, leather and tableware. Many Swazis live in poverty in the countryside. The country's workforce has been adversely affected by AIDS and life expectancy has dropped dramatically.

Quick facts:
Area: 6,704 square miles (17,364 square
    kilometres)
Population: 1,136,000
Capital: Mbabane
Other towns: Big Bend, Manzini, Mankayane,
    Lobamba
Form of government: Absolute Monarchy
Religions: Christianity, Islam, traditional beliefs
Currency: Lilangeni

Sweden

A large country in northern Europe that makes up half the Scandinavian peninsula. It stretches from the Baltic Sea north to well within the Arctic Circle. The south is generally flat with many lakes, the north mountainous and along the coast there are over 20,000 islands and islets. Summers are warm but short while winters are long and cold. In the north snow may lie for four to seven months. Dairy farming is the predominant agricultural activity and also the production of livestock, including cattle, pigs and sheep. Only 7 per cent of Sweden is cultivated, with the emphasis on fodder crops, potatoes, rape seed, grain and sugar beet. About 57 per cent of the country is covered by forest and the sawmill, wood pulp and paper industries are all of great importance. Sweden is one of the world's leading producers of iron ore, most of which is extracted from within the Arctic Circle. Other main industries are engineering and electrical goods, motor vehicles and furniture making, as well as fine crafts such as glassware, ceramics, silverware and items made from stainless steel. Sweden has an advanced social welfare system and its citizens enjoy a high standard of living. The country is known for its neutrality and although a member of the European Union it is not a member of Nato.

Quick facts:
Area: 173,732 square miles (449,964 square
   kilometres)
Population: 8,843,000
Capital: Stockholm
Other cities: Göteborg, Malmö, Uppsala,
   Örebro, Linköping
Form of government: Constitutional Monarchy
Religion: Lutheranism
Currency: Swedish Krona

Switzerland

A landlocked country in central Europe, sharing its borders with FRANCE, ITALY, AUSTRIA, LIECHTENSTEIN and GERMANY. It is still not a member of the European Union, retaining its long-standing neutral status. The Alps occupy over 70 per cent of the country's area, forming two main east-west chains divided by the Rivers Rhine and Rhône. The climate is either continental or mountain type. Summers are generally warm and winters cold and both are affected by altitude. Northern Switzerland is the industrial part of the country and where its most important cities are located. Basle is famous for its pharmaceuticals and Zürich for electrical engineering and machinery. Although the country has to import much of its raw materials, these become high-value exports such as clocks, watches and other precision engineering products. It is also in this region that the famous cheeses and chocolates are produced. Hydroelectricity accounts for approximately 60 per cent of its power supplies, with most of the remainder coming from nuclear power plants. Switzerland has huge earnings from international finance and tourism.

Quick facts:
Area: 15,940 square miles (41,284 square
    kilometres)
Population: 7,523,000
Capital: Bern
Other cities: Zürich, Basle, Geneva, Lausanne
Form of government: Federal Republic
Religions: Roman Catholicism, Protestantism
Currency: Swiss Franc

Syria (the Syrian Arab Republic)

A country in southwest Asia that borders on the Mediterranean Sea in the west. Much of the country is mountainous behind the narrow fertile coastal plain. The eastern region is desert or semi-desert, a stony inhospitable land. The coast has a Mediterranean climate, with hot dry summers and mild wet winters. About 50 per cent of the workforce get their living from agriculture: sheep, goats and cattle are raised; and cotton, barley, wheat, tobacco, grapes, olives and vegetables are grown, although some land is unused because of lack of irrigation. Reserves of oil are small compared to neighbouring IRAQ, but it has enough to make the country self-sufficient and provide three-quarters of the nation's export earnings. Industries such as textiles, food processing and phosphate rock mining have developed with the country's crafts-men producing fine rugs and silk brocades. In the 1967 Arab–Israeli War, Syria lost the Golan Heights to Israel. Despite peace talks between the two countries, the Golan Heights remain un-der Israeli control. Syria has experienced periods of political un-rest due in part to the many diverse ethnic and religious groups in its country.

Quick facts:

Area: 71,498 square miles (185,180 square kilometres)
Population: 18,881,000
Capital: Damascus (Dimashq)
Other cities: Halab, Hims, Dar'a
Form of government: Republic
Religion: Sunni Islam
Currency: Syrian Pound

Taiwan

An island that straddles the Tropic of Cancer in East Asia. It lies about 100 miles (161 kilometres) off the southeast coast of mainland CHINA. It is predominantly mountainous in the interior, with more than 60 peaks attaining heights of 10,000 feet (3,040 metres). The highest of all is the Jade Mountain (Yu Shan) which stands at 12,960 feet (3,940 metres). Taiwan's independence, resulting from the island's seizure by nationalists in 1949, is not fully accepted internationally and China lays claim to the territory. The climate is warm and humid for most of the year and winters are mild with summers rainy. The soils are fertile and a wide range of crops, including tea, rice, sugar cane and bananas, is grown. Natural resources include gas, marble, limestone and small coal deposits. Taiwan is a major international trading nation with some of the most successful export-processing zones in the world, accommodating domestic and overseas companies. Exports include machinery, electronics, textiles, footwear, toys and sporting goods.

Quick facts:
Area: 13,800 square miles (35,742 square kilometres)
Population: 23,036,000
Capital: T'ai-pei
Other cities: Kao-hsiung, T'ai-nan, Chang-hua, Chi-lung
Form of government: Multiparty Democracy
Religions: Taoism, Buddhism, Christianity
Currency: New Taiwan Dollar

Tajikistan

A republic of southern central former USSR that declared itself independent in 1991. It is situated near the Afghani and Chinese borders. The south is occupied by the Pamir mountain range, whose snow-capped peaks dominate the country. More than half the country lies over 9,840 feet (3,000 metres). Most of the country is desert or semi-desert and pastoral farming of cattle, sheep, horses and goats is important. Some yaks are kept in the higher regions. The lowland areas in the Fergana and Amudarya valleys are irrigated so that cotton, mulberry trees, fruit, wheat and vegetables can be grown. The Amudarya river is also used to produce hydroelectricity for industries such as cotton and silk processing. The republic is rich in deposits of coal, lead, zinc, oil and uranium, which were being exploited. The country's civil war in which tens of thousands of people have been killed or made homeless began soon after independence and continued until 1997. Tajikistan relies on RUSSIA's help to keep the country stable and secure as well as to improve its poor economic situation.

Quick facts:

Area: 55,250 square miles (143,100 square kilometres)
Population: 7,320,000
Capital: Dushanbe
Other major city: Khujand
Form of government: Republic
Religion: Sunni Islam, Shia Islam
Currency: Tajikistani Somoni

Tanzania

A country that lies on the east coast of central Africa and comprises a large mainland area and the islands of Pemba and Zanzibar. The mainland consists mostly of plateaus broken by mountainous areas and the East African section of the Great Rift Valley. The climate is very varied and is controlled largely by altitude and distance from the sea. The coast is hot and humid, the central plateau drier and the mountains semi-temperate. Eighty per cent of Tanzanians make a living from the land, producing corn, cassava, millet, rice, plantains and sorghum for home consumption. Cash crops include cotton, tobacco, tea, sisal, cashews and coffee. The two islands produce the bulk of the world's needs of cloves. Diamond mining is an important industry and there are also sizable deposits of iron ore, coal and tin. Fishing is also important with the bulk of the catch caught in inland waters. Tanzania's wealth of natural wonders, such as the Serengeti Plain and its wildlife, the Ngorongoro Crater, Mount Kilimanjaro and the Olduvai Gorge, attract large numbers of tourists, making a significant contribution to the country's economy. Although Tanzania is one of the poorest countries in the world, it has managed to attract some foreign investment and its annual growth rate over recent years has made it one of the best performers in sub-Saharan Africa.

Quick facts:

Area: 362,162 square miles (938,000 square kilometres)

Population: 37,445,000

Capital: Dodoma

Other towns: Dar es Salaam, Zanzibar, Mwanza, Tanga

Form of government: Republic

Religions: Sunni Islam, Roman Catholicism, Anglicanism, Hinduism

Currency: Tanzanian Shilling

Thailand

A country about the same size as FRANCE, located in Southeast Asia. It is a tropical country of mountains and jungles, rainforests and green plains. Central Thailand is a densely populated, fertile plain and the mountainous Isthmus of Kra joins southern Thailand to MALAYSIA. Thailand has a subtropical climate, with heavy monsoon rains from June to October, a cool season from October to March and a hot season from March to June. It is rich in many natural resources, such as mineral deposits of gold, coal, lead and precious stones, with rich soils, extensive areas of tropical forests and natural gas offshore. The central plain of Thailand contains vast expanses of paddy fields that grow enough rice to rank Thailand as one of the world's leading producers. The narrow southern peninsula is very wet and it is here that rubber is produced. Other crops grown are cassava, maize, pineapples and sugar cane. Tourism makes a large contribution to the country's economy. The industrial and service industries began to expand thanks to the rapidly growing economy of the 1980s and although badly affected by the 1997 southeast Asian financial crisis, the economy is now fully recovered with strong export growth. The country faces unrest in its southern provinces where a minority Muslim population has renewed its separatist struggle.

Quick facts:
Area: 198,115 square miles (513,115 square
   kilometres)
Population: 64,631,000
Capital: Bangkok (Krung Thep)
Other cities: Chiang Mai, Nakhon Ratchasima,
   Ubon Ratchathani
Form of government: Constitutional Monarchy
Religions: Buddhism, Sunni Islam
Currency: Baht

Togo

A tiny country with a narrow coastal plain on the Gulf of Guinea in West Africa. Grassy plains in the north and south are separated by the Togo Highlands (2,300–3,235 feet/700–986 metres), which run from southwest to northeast. High plateaus, mainly in the more southerly ranges, are heavily forested with teak, mahogany and bamboo. Wildlife species are varied and include birds, monkeys, snakes, crocodiles, hippopotamus, antelope and lion. Togo has a tropical climate with a major rainy season from March to July and a minor one from October to November. The north is affected by the dry harmattan wind from the Sahara during December and January. Over 80 per cent of the population is involved in subsistence agriculture, with yams, cassava, sorghum and millet as the principal crops. Minerals, particularly phosphates, are now the main export earners, along with raw cotton, coffee, cocoa, cement and palm kernels. Ongoing political unrest continues to weaken the economy.

Quick facts:
Area: 21,925 square miles (56,785 square kilometres)
Population: 5,548,000
Capital: Lomé
Other major city: Sokodé
Form of government: Republic
Religions: Traditional beliefs, Roman Catholicism, Sunni Islam
Currency: CFA Franc

Tonga

A country situated about 20 degrees south of the equator and just west of the International Date Line in the Pacific Ocean. It comprises over 170 islands, only about 40 of which are inhabited. It comprises a low limestone chain of islands in the east and a higher volcanic chain in the west. The climate is warm with heavy rainfall, and destructive cyclones are likely to occur every few years. The government owns all the land, and males can rent an allotment for growing food. Yams, cassava and taro are grown as subsistence crops, and fish from the sea supplement the diet while foods such as pumpkins, bananas, vanilla and coconuts are exported. The main industry is coconut processing. About 70 per cent of the workforce is occupied in either fishing or agriculture while many Tongans are employed overseas. Tourism, foreign aid from countries such as the United Kingdom, Australia and New Zealand and the income sent home from overseas workers all contribute to the country's economy.

Quick facts:
Area: 288 square miles (747 square kilometres)
Population: 114,000
Capital: Nuku'alofa
Form of government: Constitutional Monarchy
Religions: Methodism, Roman Catholicism
Currency: Pa'anga

Trinidad and Tobago

The islands constitute the third largest British Commonwealth country in the West Indies and are situated off the Orinoco Delta in northeastern VENEZUELA. They are the most southerly of the Lesser Antilles. Trinidad consists of the mountainous Northern Range in the north and undulating plains in the south. It has a huge, asphalt-producing lake, Pitch Lake, which is approximately 104 acres (42 hectares) in size. Tobago is actually a mountain that is about 1,800 feet (550 metres) above sea level at its peak. The climate is tropical with little variation in temperatures throughout the year and a rainy season from June to December. Trinidad is one of the oldest oil-producing countries in the world. Output is small but provides 90 per cent of Trinidad's exports. Sugar cane, cocoa, citrus fruits, vegetables and rubber trees are grown for export, but imports of food now account for 10 per cent of total imports. Tobago depends mainly on tourism for revenue but this has been threatened recently by increasing levels of crime in the country. A slump in the economy in the 1980s and early 1990s saw widespread unemployment but economic growth has improved in recent times and the country remains one of the most prosperous in the Caribbean.

Quick facts:
Area: 1,981 square miles (5,130 square kilometres)
Population: 1,065,000
Capital: Port of Spain
Other towns: San Fernando, Arima
Form of government: Parliamentary Democracy
Religions: Roman Catholicism, Hinduism, Anglicanism, Sunni Islam
Currency: Trinidad and Tobago Dollar

Tunisia

A North African country that lies on the south coast of the Mediterranean Sea. It is bounded by ALGERIA to the west and LIBYA to the south. Northern Tunisia consists of hills, plains and valleys. Inland mountains separate the coastal zone from the central plains before the land drops down to an area of salt pans and the Sahara. The climate ranges from warm temperate in the north, where there are vineyards and forests of pine, cork oak and junipers, to desert in the south. Agriculture produces wheat, barley, olives, grapes, tomatoes, dates, vegetables and citrus fruits and the fishing industry is of growing importance, producing mainly pilchards, sardines and tuna. Twenty-six per cent of the workforce is engaged in these two occupations, but overall there is a general lack of employment. The mainstay of Tunisia's modern economy, however, is oil from the Sahara, phosphates, natural gas and tourism on the Mediterranean coast. Tourists are attracted by the good beaches and historic sites such as the ancient city of Carthage.

Quick facts:

Area: 62,592 square miles (162,155 square kilometres)
Population: 10,175,000
Capital: Tunis
Other cities: Sfax, Bizerte, Sousse
Form of government: Republic
Religion: Sunni Islam
Currency: Tunisian Dinar

Turkey

With land on the continents of Europe and Asia, Turkey forms
a bridge between the two. It guards the sea passage between
the Mediterranean and the Black Sea. Turkey occupies an area
in which seismic activity is a frequent occurrence and the country regularly experiences devastating earthquakes. Only 5 per
cent of its area, Thrace, is in Europe and the much larger area,
Anatolia, is in Asia. European Turkey is fertile agricultural land
with a Mediterranean climate. Asiatic Turkey is bordered to the
north by the Pontine Mountains and to the south by the Taurus
Mountains. The climate here ranges from Mediterranean to hot
summers and bitterly cold winters in the central plains. Agriculture employs almost half the workforce, with the major crops
being wheat, sugar beet, barley, fruits, maize and oil seeds. The
country's main exports are iron and steel, textiles, dried fruits,
tobacco, leather clothes and petroleum products. Manufacturing
industry includes iron and steel, textiles, motor vehicles and Turkey's famous carpets. The main mineral resources are iron ore,
coal, chromium, magnetite, zinc and lead. Hydroelectric power is
supplied by the Tigris and Euphrates. Tourism is a fast-developing
industry and plays an increasingly important role in the economy.
The economy has been growing in strength but foreign debt is
still a burden. Turkey became a European Union candidate country in 1999 and membership talks began in 2005.

Quick facts:
Area: 299,158 square miles (774,815 square
   kilometres)
Population: 70,413,000
Capital: Ankara
Other cities: Istanbul, Izmir, Adana, Bursa
Form of government: Republic
Religion: Sunni Islam
Currency: New Turkish Lira

Turkmenistan

A central Asian republic of the former USSR that declared itself a republic in 1991. It lies to the east of the Caspian Sea and borders IRAN and AFGHANISTAN to the south. Much of the west and central areas of Turkmenistan are covered by the sandy Karakum Kum. The east is a plateau that is bordered by the Amudarya river. The Amudarya has been diverted to form the important Kara Kum Canal which is one of the longest canals in the world and provides irrigation and drinking water for the southeastern parts of the country. The climate is extremely dry, and most of the population live in oasis settlements near the rivers and by the extensive network of canals. Agriculture is intensive around the settlements and consists of growing cotton, cereals, silk, fruit and rearing Karakul sheep. This occupies around 45 per cent of the workforce. There are rich mineral deposits, particularly natural gas, petroleum, sulphur, coal, salt and copper. There is some industry, such as textile manufacturing, food processing and carpet weaving. Unlike most other former Soviet republics, there has not been a wholesale emigration of ethnic minorities. The economy remains largely underdeveloped and the country largely closed to the outside world.

Quick facts:
Area: 188,456 square miles (488,100 square
    kilometres)
Population: 5,042,000
Capital: Ashkhabad (Ashgabat)
Other cities: Chardzhou, Mary, Turkmenbashi
Form of government: Republic
Religion: Sunni Islam, Eastern Orthodox
Currency: Turkmen Manat

Turks and Caicos Islands

Two island groups which form the southeastern archipelago of the Bahamas in the Atlantic Ocean. Only six of the islands are inhabited. A British Overseas Territory, the country's economy relies mainly on tourism and offshore finance. The climate is subtropical cooled by southeast trade winds which blow all the year round. The territory also enjoys strong links with Canada.

Quick facts:
Area: 166 square miles (430 square kilometres)
Population: 21,152
Capital: Grand Turk
Form of government: British Overseas Territory
Religion: Christianity
Currency: US Dollar

Tuvalu

A country located just north of Fiji, in the South Pacific, consisting of nine coral atolls. The group was formerly known as the Ellice Islands, and the main island and capital is Funafuti. Tuvalu became independent in 1978. The climate is tropical, with an annual average rainfall of 120 inches (3,050 millimetres). Coconut palms are the main crop and fruit and vegetables are grown for local consumption. Sea fishing is extremely good and licences have been sold to Japan, Taiwan and the Republic of Korea to fish the local waters. Revenue also comes from copra (the only export product), foreign aid, the sale of elaborate postage stamps to philatelists and income sent home from Tuvaluans who work abroad.

Quick facts:

Area: 10 square miles (24 square kilometres)
Population: 11,810
Capital: Funafuti
Form of government: Constitutional Monarchy
Religion: Christianity
Currency: Tuvaluan Dollar/Australian Dollar

Uganda

A landlocked country in east central Africa. The equator runs through the south of the country and for the most part it is a richly fertile land, well watered, with a kindly climate. In the west are the Ruwenzori Mountains, which reach heights of 16,762 feet (5,109 metres) and are snow-capped. The lowlands around Lake Victoria, once forested, have now mostly been cleared for cultivation. Agriculture employs over 80 per cent of the labour force and the main crops grown for subsistence are plantains, cassava and sweet potatoes. Coffee is the main cash crop and accounts for over 90 per cent of the country's exports although cotton and tea are important. Attempts are being made to expand the tea plantations in the west, to develop a copper mine and to introduce new industries to Kampala, the capital. Forestry is of importance, with the major export being mahogany, while the bulk of other wood is used as fuel. Virtually all the country's power is produced by hydroelectricity, the plant on the Victoria Nile being of major importance. Since 1986, Uganda has slowly rebuilt its shattered economy after years of civil war and is now relatively stable.

Quick facts:
Area: 93,065 square miles (241,038 square
  kilometres)
Population: 28,195,000
Capital: Kampala
Other cities: Entebbe, Jinja, Soroti, Mbale
Form of government: Republic
Religions: Roman Catholicism, Protestantism,
  traditional beliefs, Sunni Islam
Currency: Ugandan Shilling

Ukraine

A former Soviet socialist republic that declared itself independent of the former USSR in 1991. Its neighbours to the west are POLAND, SLOVAKIA, HUNGARY and ROMANIA, and it is bounded to the south by the Black Sea. To the east lies RUSSIA and to the north the republic of BELARUS. Drained by the Dnepr, Dnestr, Southern Bug AND Donets rivers, Ukraine consists largely of fertile steppes. The climate is continental, although this is greatly modified by the proximity of the Black Sea. The Ukrainian steppe is one of the chief wheat-producing regions of Europe. Other major crops include corn, sugar beet, flax, tobacco, soya, hops and potatoes, with agriculture accounting for about a quarter of all employment. There are rich reserves of coal and raw materials for industry, but the country is still reliant on Russia for natural gas and oil. The central and eastern regions form one of the world's densest industrial concentrations. Manufacturing industries include ferrous metallurgy, heavy machinery, chemicals, food processing, gas and oil refining. In 1986 the catastrophic accident at the Chernobyl nuclear power station occurred, which had far-reaching effects and caused widespread contamination. The amount of trade with European Union countries is now greater than that with Russia and Ukraine hopes to be a member of the EU by 2015.

Quick facts:

Area: 233,090 square miles (603,700 square kilometres)
Population: 51,094,000
Capital: Kiev (Kiyev)
Other cities: Dnepropetrovsk, Donetsk, Khar'kov, Odessa, Lugansk, Sevastopol
Form of government: Republic
Religions: Russian Orthodox, Roman Catholicism
Currency: Rouble

United Arab Emirates (UAE)

A federation of seven oil-rich sheikdoms located in the Gulf: Abu Dhabi, Dubai, Ajman, Fujairah, Ras al Khaimah, Sharjah and Umm al Qaiwain. As well as its main coast on the Gulf, the country has a short coast on the Gulf of Oman. The land is mainly flat sandy desert except to the north on the peninsula where the Hajar Mountains rise to 6,828 feet (2,081 metres). The summers are hot and humid with temperatures reaching 120°F (49°C), but from October to May the weather is warm and sunny with pleasant, cool evenings. The only fertile areas are the emirate of Ras al Khaimah, the coastal plain of Fujairah and the oases. Abu Dhabi and Dubai are the main industrial centres and, using their wealth from the oil industry, they are now diversifying industry by building aluminium smelters, cement factories and steel-rolling mills. The country's growing business sector and tourist industry have led to a construction boom with many showpiece buildings. Prior to development of the oil industry, traditional occupations were pearl diving, growing dates, fishing and camel breeding. Dubai is the richest state in the world.

Quick facts:
Area: 32,278 square miles (83,600 square kilometres)
Population: 2,602,000
Capital: Abu Zabi (Abu Dhabi)
Form of government: Federation
Religion: Sunni Islam, Shia Islam
Currency: Emirati Dirham

United Kingdom of Great Britain and Northern Ireland (UK)

A country situated in northwest Europe, comprising the island of Great Britain (England, Wales and Scotland) and the six counties of Northern Ireland, plus many smaller islands, especially off the west coast of Scotland. The south and east of Britain is low-lying, and the Pennines form a backbone running through northern England. Scotland has the largest area of upland, and Wales is a highland block. Northern Ireland has a few hilly areas. The climate is cool temperate with mild conditions and an even annual rainfall. The UK is primarily a highly urbanised industrial and commercial country. Only 2 per cent of the workforce are employed in agriculture and, although production is high thanks to modern machinery and scientific methods, the UK still has to import one third of its food. Major crops include barley, potatoes, sugar beet and wheat, while livestock raised includes sheep, cattle, pigs and poultry. Fishing is also an important industry. The UK's natural resources include coal, iron ore, oil and natural gas. Many of the older industries, such as the coal, textiles and heavy engineering industries, have declined significantly in recent years while service industries play an increasingly large part in the UK's economy, as does tourism. The UK has played an important role in the EU, UN and Nato.

Quick facts:

Area: 94,248 square miles (244,101 square kilometres)

Population: 60,609,000

Capital: London

Other cities: Birmingham, Manchester, Glasgow, Liverpool, Edinburgh, Cardiff, Belfast

Form of government: Constitutional Monarchy

Religions: Christianity, Islam, Hinduism, Judaism

Currency: Pound Sterling

United States of America (USA)

A country that stretches across central north America, from the Atlantic Ocean in the east to the Pacific Ocean in the west, and from CANADA in the north to MEXICO and the Gulf of Mexico in the south. It is the fourth largest country in the world and consists of fifty states, including outlying Alaska, northwest of Canada, and Hawaii in the Pacific Ocean. The climate varies a great deal in such a large country. In Alaska there are polar conditions, and in the Gulf coast and in Florida conditions may be subtropical. The highest point is Mount McKinley at 20,322 feet (6,194 metres). Natural resources include vast mineral reserves, including oil and gas, coal, copper, lead, uranium gold, tungsten and lumber. Although agricultural production is high, it employs only 1.5 per cent of the population because primarily of its advanced technology. The USA is a world leader in oil production. The main industries are iron and steel, chemicals, motor vehicles, aircraft, telecommunications equipment, computers, electronics and textiles. The USA is the richest and most powerful nation in the world. The terrorist attacks of September 2001 have caused the country to look again at its role as the world's only superpower, with military campaigns in Afghanistan and Iraq as part of its 'war on terror'.

Quick facts:
Area: 3,536,278 square miles (9,158,960 square kilometres)
Population: 298,444,000
Capital: Washington DC
Other cities: New York, Chicago, Detroit, Houston, Los Angeles, Philadelphia, San Diego, San Francisco
Form of government: Federal Republic
Religions: Christianity, Judaism, Eastern Orthodox, Islam
Currency: US Dollar

Uruguay

One of the smallest countries in South America. It lies on the east coast of the continent, to the south of BRAZIL and is bordered to the west by the Uruguay river, Rio de la Plata to the south and the Atlantic Ocean to the east. The country consists of low plains and plateaus. The Negro river, which rises in Brazil, crosses the country from northeast to southwest, dividing Uruguay almost into two halves. The climate is temperate and rainfall plentiful and the natural vegetation is prairie grassland. Some of the river valleys are wooded but Uruguay lacks the dense forests of other parts of South America. About 90 per cent of the land is suitable for agriculture but only about 8 per cent is cultivated, the remainder being used to graze the vast herds of cattle and sheep that provide over 35 per cent of Uruguay's exports in the form of wool, hides and meat. The cultivated land is made up of vineyards, rice fields and groves of olives and citrus fruits. The main crops grown are sugar beet and cane, rice, wheat, potatoes, corn and sorghum. The country has scarce mineral resources and hydroelectric power supplies most of its energy needs. Industries include textile manufacture, food processing, oil refining, steel, aluminium, electrical goods and rubber. The country is still recovering from economic problems experienced in 2002.

Quick facts:

Area: 68,500 square miles (177,414 square kilometres)
Population: 3,431,000
Capital: Montevideo
Form of government: Republic
Religions: Roman Catholicism, Protestantism
Currency: Uruguayan Peso

Uzbekistan

A central Asian republic of the former USSR that declared itself independent in 1991. It lies between KAZAKHSTAN and TURKMENISTAN and encompasses the southern half of the Aral Sea. The republic has many contrasting regions. The Tian Shan region is mountainous, the Fergana region is irrigated and fertile, the Kyzlkum Desert (one of the world's largest) is rich in oil and gas, the lower Amudarya river region is irrigated and has oasis settlements and the Usturt Plateau is a stony desert. Uzbekistan is one of the world's leading cotton producers and Karakul lambs are reared for wool and meat. Its main industrial products are agricultural machinery, textiles and chemicals. It also has significant reserves of natural gas. Economic growth has been checked by concerns about political instability and much of the economy remains based on the centralised state-owned model. There are serious pollution problems where the Aral Sea lies. This has greatly decreased in size from its use for irrigation and is contaminated with toxins, salts and sands that poison the water supply of the surrounding population. Hydroelectric schemes supply much of the republic's electricity needs. Povety and unemployment are widespread and economic reform is needed if the country is to take advantage of its rich natural resources. The country considers RUSSIA to be its greatest ally.

Quick facts:
Area: 172,742 square miles (447,400 square kilometres)
Population: 27,307,000
Capital: Tashkent
Other cities: Urgench, Nukus, Bukhara, Samarkand
Form of government: Republic
Religion: Sunni Islam, Eastern Othodox
Currency: Uzbekistani Soum

Vanuatu

A country, formerly known as the New Hebrides (so named by Captain Cook in 1774), located in the southwest Pacific Ocean, southeast of the SOLOMON ISLANDS and about 1,087 miles (1,750 kilometres) east of AUSTRALIA.

It consists of some 12 islands and 60 islets. Most of the islands are volcanic and densely forested, with raised coral beaches and fringed by coral reefs. The largest islands are Espírtu Santo, Malekula and Efate, on which the capital, Vila, is sited. Vanuatu has a tropical climate that is moderated by the southeast trade winds from May to October. Cultivated land is generally restricted to the coastal plains and the main cash crops are copra, cocoa beans and coffee. Meat and fish are also exported and light industries include food processing and handicrafts for an increasing tourist industry. The majority of the labour force is engaged in subsistence farming, raising taro, yams and bananas. Eco-tourism is becoming important. Vanuatu receives most of its foreign aid from Australia who are encouraging economic reform.

Quick facts:

Area: 4,706 square miles (12,189 square
  kilometres)
Population: 208, 869
Capital: Vila
Form of government: Republic
Religion: Roman Catholicism, traditional beliefs
Currency: Vatu

Vatican City State

A state, established in 1929, that lies in the heart of Rome on a low hill on the west bank of the River Tiber. It is the world's smallest independent state and headquarters of the Roman Catholic Church. It is a walled city with six gates and is made up of the Vatican Palace, the Papal Gardens, St Peter's Square and St Peter's Basilica. The state has its own police, newspaper, telephone and telegraph services, coinage, stamps, radio station and train station. The radio station, Radio Vaticana, broadcasts a service in 34 languages from transmitters within the Vatican City. Its main tourist attractions are the frescoes of the Sistine Chapel, painted by Michelangelo Buonarroti. It also has outstanding museums, with collections of antiquities and works by Italian masters and the Vatican Library's collection of ancient manuscripts is priceless. The pope exercises sovereignty and has absolute legislative, executive and judicial powers.

Quick facts:
Area: 0.2 square miles (0.44 square kilometres)
Population: 1,000
Capital: Vatican City
Form of government: Papal Commission
Religion: Roman Catholicism
Currency: Euro

Venezuela

A country that forms the northernmost crest of South America. Its northern coast lies along the Caribbean Sea and it is bounded to the west by COLUMBIA and to the southeast and south by GUYANA and BRAZIL. In the northwest a spur of the Andes runs southwest to northeast. Venezuela has one of the highest waterfalls in the world, the Angel Falls. The River Orinoco cuts the country in two and north of the river run the undulating plains known as the Llanos. South of the river are the Guiana Highlands. The climate ranges from warm temperate to tropical. Temperatures vary little throughout the year and rainfall is plentiful. In the Llanos area, cattle are herded across the plains and this region makes the country almost self-sufficient in meat. There are also rich fishing grounds around the coast and off Venezuela's 72 islands. Sugar cane and coffee are grown for export, but petroleum and gas account for around 80 per cent of export earnings. Venezuela's economy is built on its oilfields located in the Maracaibo region but it also has other important mineral reserves including bauxite, iron ore; coal and precious metals and stones, such as gold, silver, platinum and diamonds. Despite this wealth of natural resources, most of the population live in poverty and unemployment is high. Recently the economy has been adversely affected by political unrest.

Quick facts:

Area: 352,145 square miles (912,050 square kilometres)
Population: 25,730,000
Capital: Caracas
Other cities: Maracaibo, Valencia, Barquisimeto
Form of government: Federal Republic
Religion: Roman Catholicism
Currency: Bolivar

Vietnam

A long narrow country in Southeast Asia that runs down the coast of the South China Sea. It has a narrow central area that links broader plains centred on the Red (Hong) and Mekong rivers. The narrow zone, now known as Mien Trung, is hilly and makes communications between north and south difficult. The climate is humid, with tropical conditions in the south and subtropical in the north. The far north can be very cold when polar air blows over Asia. Agriculture, fishing and forestry employ around 74 per cent of the labour force. The main crop is rice but cassava, maize and sweet potatoes are also grown for domestic consumption. Soya beans, tea, coffee and rubber are grown for export. Major industries are food processing, textiles, cement, cotton and silk manufacture. Fishing is also an important export trade that is conducted mainly on the South China Sea, although there is some fish farming in flooded inland areas. Vietnam, still recovering from the ravages of many wars this century, is now one of southeast Asia's fastest growing economies. Foreign investment has grown and a stock exchange was opened in 2000.

Quick facts:
Area: 128,066 square miles (331,689 square kilometres)
Population: 84,402,000
Capital: Hanoi
Other cities: Ho Chi Minh City, Haiphong, Hué, Dà Nang
Form of government: Socialist Republic
Religions: Buddhism, Taoism, Roman Catholicism
Currency: Dong

Virgin Islands, British

A British Overseas Territory lying at the northwestern end of the Lesser Antilles in the Caribbean Sea. They comprise four large islands and 36 islets and cays. Only 16 of the islands are inhabited. Most of the islands are hilly and wooded and the climate is subtropical moderated by trade winds. Agriculture produces livestock, coconuts, sugar cane, fruit and vegetables, but only a small percentage of the land available to agriculture is under cultivation. The main industries are tourism and offshore finance and these dominate the economy.

Quick facts:
Area: 58 square miles (151 square kilometres)
Population: 23,000
Capital: Road Town
Form of government: British Overseas Territory
Religion: Protestantism
Currency: US Dollar

Virgin Islands, US

Part of the Virgin Islands group in the northwest of the Lesser Antilles in the Caribbean Sea. A self-governing US territory, this group of 50 volcanic islands are rugged and mountainous with a subtropical climate. The main islands are St John (around two-thirds of which is a National Park), St Croix and St Thomas. Agriculture is not well developed and most of the country's food has to be imported. There is a small manufacturing industry but tourism is the mainstay of the economy with many cruise ships calling at the island of St Thomas because of its natural deep-water harbour.

Quick facts:

Area: 134 square miles (347 square kilometres)
Population: 108,000
Capital: Charlotte Amalie
Form of government: Self-governing US Territory
Religion: Baptist, Roman Catholicism
Currency: US Dollar

Wallis and Futuna Islands

The two island groups are 142 miles (230 kilometres) apart in the southern central Pacific Ocean and are the smallest and poorest of France's overseas territories. The climate is warm and humid with a cyclone season between October and March. Subsistence farming and fishing are the main activities with copra the only important export.

Quick facts:
Area: 77 square miles (200 square
    kilometres)
Population: 16,000
Capital: Mata-Uru
Form of government: French Overseas
    Territory
Religion: Roman Catholicism
Currency: CFP Franc

Western Sahara

A disputed territory of western Africa, with a coastline on the Atlantic Ocean. Consisting mainly of desert, it is rich in phosphates. It was a Spanish overseas province until 1976, when it was partitioned between MOROCCO and MAURITANIA. Since 1979, the entire territory has been claimed and administered by Morocco, against the wishes of an active separatist movement, the Frente Polisario. Moroccan sovereignty is not universally recognised and the United Nations has attempted to oversee a referendum to decide the struggle but without success so far. It is a poor country with many following a nomadic existence. The bulk of the food for the towns has to be imported. Phosphates comprise two-thirds of the meagre exports.

Quick facts:
Area: 102,703 square miles (266,000 square kilometres)
Population: 273,000
Capital: Laâyoune (El Aaiún)
Form of government: Republic (de facto controlled by Morocco)
Religion: Sunni Islam
Currency: Moroccan Dirham

Western Samoa see SAMOA.

Yemen

A country bounded by SAUDI ARABIA in the north, OMAN in the east, the Gulf of Aden in the south and the Red Sea in the west. The country was formed after the unification of the previous Yemen Arab Republic and the People's Democratic Republic of Yemen (South Yemen) in 1990. At that point, however, there was no active integration of the two countries and politically the country remained divided between north and south. In 1994 a civil war that lasted three months broke out between the former North Yemen and South Yemen, which resulted in defeat for the southern separatists and a high rate of inflation, damage to the infrastructure and devaluation of the currency. Most of the country comprises rugged mountains and trackless desert lands. The country is almost entirely dependent on agriculture even although only a very small percentage is fertile. The main crops are coffee, cotton, wheat, vegetables, millet, sorghum and fruit. Fishing is an important industry, with mackerel, tuna, lobster and cod being caught and there are some canning factories along the coast. Other industry is on a very small scale, consisting mainly of manufacturing industry which produces textiles, paints, matches, plastic, rubber and aluminium goods. Modernisation is slow because of a lack of funds and economic problems have caused unrest.

Quick facts:

Area: 203,850 square miles (527,978 square kilometres)
Population: 21,456,000
Capital: San'a
Commercial *Capital:* Aden (Adan)
Other cities: Al Hudaydah, Ta'izz
Form of government: Republic
Religions: Sunni Islam, Shia Islam
Currency: Yemeni Riyal

Zambia

A country, situated in central Africa, that is made up of high plateaus. Bordering it to the south is the Zambezi river and in the southwest it borders on the Kalahari Desert. It has some other large rivers, including the Luangwa, and lakes, the largest of which is Lake Bangweulu. The climate is tropical, modified somewhat by altitude. The country has a wide range of wildlife and there are large game parks on the Luangwa and Kafue rivers. Agriculture is underdeveloped and vulnerable to weather variations, leading to some food shortages, as a consequence of which large quantities have to be imported. The principal subsistence crops grown are corn, sugar cane and cassava, with cattle raised and most foodstuffs have to be imported. The majority of the country's power is provided by the Kariba Dam on the Zambezi river. Zambia's economy relies heavily on the mining of copper, lead, zinc and cobalt. The World Bank has encouraged Zambia to develop her vast agricultural potential and tourism but copper still accounts for most of the country's foreign earnings.

Quick facts:
Area: 290,587 square miles (752,618 square
    kilometres)
Population: 11,502,000
Capital: Lusaka
Other cities: Kitwe, Ndola, Mufulira
Form of government: Republic
Religions: Christianity, traditional beliefs, Islam
Currency: Zambian Kwacha

Zaire *see* Congo, Democratic Republic of the.

Zimbabwe

A landlocked country in southern Africa. It is a country with spectacular physical features and is teeming with wildlife. It is bordered in the north by the Zambezi river, which flows over the mile-wide Victoria Falls before entering Lake Kariba. In the south, the River Limpopo marks its border with SOUTH AFRICA. A great plateau between 4,000–5,000 feet (about 1,200–1,500 metres) in height occupies the central area. The climate is tropical in the lowlands and subtropical in the higher land. Zimbabwe is rich in mineral resources such as coal, chromium, nickel, gold, platinum and precious metals. Tourism has the potential to be a major growth industry. However, during the years of President Mugabe's rule, the agriculture-based economy has collapsed after the forced seizure of white-owned commercial farms, and the country has had to put up with a very high inflation rate, high unemployment and political unrest.

Quick facts:

Area: 150,872 square miles (390,757 square kilometres)
Population: 12,236,000
Capital: Harare
Other cities: Bulawayo, Mutare, Gweru
Form of government: Republic
Religions: Traditional beliefs, Christianity
Currency: Zimbabwean Dollar

The Earth's Statistics

Earth's Vital Statistics

Age: Approx 4600 million years

Weight: Approx 5.976×10^{21} tonnes

Diameter: Pole to Pole through the centre of the Earth 7900 miles (12,713 km) Across the Equator through the centre of the Earth 7926 miles (12,756 km)

Circumference: Around the Poles 24 861 miles (40,008 km) Around the Equator 40 091 km(24,912 miles)

Area: Land 57,268,700 sq miles (148,326,000 sq km) 29% of surface
Water 139,667,810 sq miles (361,740,000 sq km) 71% of surface

Volume: 260 160 million cubic miles (1 084 000 million cubic km)

Volume of the oceans: 317 million cubic miles (1321 million cubic km)

Average height of land: 2756 ft (840 m) above sea level

Average depth of ocean: 3808 m (12,493 ft) below sea level

Density: 5.52 times water

Mean temperature: 22°C (72°F)

Length of year: 365.25 days

Length of one rotation: 23 hours 56 minutes

Mean distance from Sun: 149,600,000 km (92 960 000 miles)

Mean velocity in orbit: 18.5 miles (29.8 km) per second

Escape velocity: 6.96 miles (11.2 km) per second

Atmosphere: Main constituents: nitrogen (78.5%), oxygen (21%)

Crust: Main constituents: oxygen (47%), silicon (28%), aluminium (8%), iron (5%)

Known satellites: One (the Moon)

Oceans

	Max. Depth		Area	
	metres	feet	sq km	sq miles
Pacific	11 033	36 197	165 384 000	63 860 000
Atlantic	8381	27 496	82,217 000	31 744 000
Indian	8047	26 401	73 481 000	28 371 000
Arctic	5450	17 880	14 056 000	5 427 000

Deserts

	sq km	sq miles
Sahara	9 065 000	3 500 000
Australian Desert	1 550 000	598 455
Arabian Desert	1 300 000	501 930
Gobi Desert	1 295 000	500 000
Kalahari	520 000	200 772

Largest Islands

Island (location)	Population	Area	
		sq km	sq miles
Greenland (N. Atlantic)	54 600	2 175 600	839 740
New Guinea (S.W. Pacific)	4 528 682	808 510	312 085
Borneo (S.W. Pacific)	11 263 087	751 900	292 220
Madagascar (Indian Ocean)	11 238 000	594 180	229 355

| Island | Population | Area | |
(location)		sq km	sq miles
Sumatra			
(Indian Ocean)	36 881 990	524 100	202 300
Baffin I.			
(Canadian Arctic)	8298	476 070	183 760
Honshu			
(N.W. Pacific)	98 352 000	230 455	88 955
Great Britain			
(N. Atlantic)	54 285 422	229 880	88 730
Victoria I.			
(Canadian Arctic)	1410	212 200	81 910
Ellesmere			
(Canadian Arctic)	54	212 690	82 100

Principal Mountains of the World

| Name | Height | |
(location)	m	ft
Everest		
(Tibet-Nepal)	8848	29 028
Godwin-Austen or K2		
(Kashmir-Sinkiang)	8611	28 250
Kangchenjunga		
(Nepal-India)	8587	28 170
Makalu		
(Nepal)	8463	27 766
Dhaulagiri		
(Nepal)	8167	26 795
Nanga Parbat		
(India)	8125	26 657
Annapurna		
(Nepal)	8091	26 545
Gosainthan		
(Tibet)	8012	26 286
Nanda Devi		
(India)	7816	25 643

| Name | Height | |
(location)	m	ft
Kamet (India)	7756	25 446
Namcha Barwa (Tibet)	7756	25 446
Gurla Mandhata (Tibet)	7728	25 355
Kongur (China)	7720	25 325
Tirich Mir (Pakistan)	7691	25 230
Minya Kanka (China)	7556	24 790
Kula Kangri (Tibet)	7555	24 784
Muztagh Ata (China)	7546	24 757
Kommunizma (Tajikistan)	7495	24 590
Pobedy (Russian Fed.-China)	7439	24 406
Chomo Lhari (Bhutan-Tibet)	7313	23 992
Api (Nepal)	7132	23 399
Lenina (Kyrgyzstan-Tajikistan)	7134	23 405
Acongagua (volcanic) (Argentina)	6960	22 834
Ojos del Salado (Argentina)	6908	22 664
Tupungato (Argentina-Chile)	6801	22 310
Mercedario (Argentina)	6770	22 211
Huascarán (Peru)	6769	22 205

Name	Height	
(location)	m	ft
Llullailaco		
(Chile)	6723	22 057
Neradas de Cachi		
(Argentina)	6720	22 047
Kailas		
(Tibet)	6714	22 027
Incahuasi		
(Argentina)	6709	22 011
Tengri Khan		
(Kyrgyzstan)	6695	21 965
Sajama		
(Bolivia)	6542	21,463
Illampu		
(Bolivia)	6485	21 276
Antofalla (volcanic)		
(Argentina)	6441	21 129
Illimani		
(Bolivia)	6402	21 004
Chimborazo (volcanic)		
(Ecuador)	6310	20 702
Cumbre de la Mejicana		
(Argentina)	6249	20 500
McKinley		
(Alaska)	6194	20 320
Copiapo or Azifre		
(Chile)	6080	19 947
Logan		
(Yukon, Canada)	6051	19 524
Cotopaxi (volcanic)		
(Ecuador)	5896	19 344
Kilimanjaro (volcanic)		
(Tanzania)	5895	19 340
Ollagüe		
(Chile-Bolivia)	5868	19 250
Cerro del Potro		
(Argentina-Chile)	5830	19 127

Name (location)	Height m	ft
Misti (volcanic) (Peru)	5822	19 101
Cayambe (Ecuador)	5797	19 016
Huila (volcanic) (Colombia)	5750	18 865
Citlaltepi (Mexico)	5699	18 697
Demavend (Iran)	5664	18 582
Elbrus (volcanic) (Russian Fed.)	5642	18 510
St Elias (volcanic) (Alaska, Canada)	5489	18 008
Popocatepetl (volcanic) (Mexico)	5453	17 887
Cerro Lejfa (Chile)	5360	17 585
Foraker (Alaska)	5304	17 400
Maipo (volcanic) (Argentina-Chile)	5290	17 355
Ixtaccihuati (volcanic) (Mexico)	5286	17 342
Lucania (Yukon, Canada)	5228	17 150
Tomila (volcanic) (Colombia)	5215	17 109
Dykh Tau (Russian Fed.)	5203	17 070
Kenya (Kenya)	5200	17 058
Ararat (Turkey)	5165	16 945
Vinson Massif (Antarctica)	5140	16 863

Name	Height	
(location)	m	ft
Kazbek (volcanic)		
(Georgia)	5047	16 558
Blackburn		
(Alaska)	5037	16 523
Jaya		
(Irian Jaya, Indonesia)	5030	16 502
Sanford		
(Alaska)	4941	16 208
Klyucheveyskava (volcanic)		
(Russian Fed.)	4750	15 584
Mont Blanc		
(France-Italy)	4808	15 774
Domuyo (volcanic)		
(Argentina)	4800	15 748
Vancouver		
(Alaska-Yukon, Canada)	4786	15 700
Trikora		
(West Irian, Indonesia)	4750	15 584
Fairweather		
(Alaska-British Colombia, Canada)	4670	15 320
Monte Rosa		
(Switzerland-Italy)	4634	15 203
Ras Dashan		
(Ethiopia)	4620	15 158
Belukha		
(Kazakhstan)	4506	14 783
Markham		
(Antarctica)	4350	14 271
Meru (volcanic)		
(Tanzania)	4566	14 979
Hubbard		
(Alaska-Yukon)	4557	14 950
Kirkpatrick		
(Antarctica)	4528	14 855
Karisimbi (volcanic)		
(Rwanda-Zaire)	4508	14 787

Name (location)	Height	
	m	ft
Weisshorn (Switzerland)	4505	14 780
Matterhorn/Mont Cervin (Switzerland-Italy)	4477	14 690
Whitney (California)	4418	14 495
Elbert (Colorado)	4399	14 431
Massive Mount (Colorado)	4397	14 424
Harvard (Colorado)	4396	14 420
Rainier or Tacoma (Washington)	4392	14 410
Williamson (California)	4382	14 375
La Plata (Colorado)	4371	14 340
Blanca Peak (Colorado)	4364	14 317
Uncompahgre (Colorado)	4361	14 306
Crestone (Colorado)	4356	14 291
Lincoln (Colorado)	4354	14 284
Grays (Colorado)	4351	14 274
Evans (Colorado)	4347	14 260
Longs (Colorado)	4345	14 255
White (California)	4343	14 246
Colima (volcanic) (Mexico)	4340	14 236

Name	Height	
(location)	m	ft
Shavano (Colorado)	4337	14 229
Princeton (Colorado)	4327	14 196
Yale (Colorado)	4327	14 196
Elgon (volcanic) (Uganda-Kenya)	4321	14 176
Shasta (volcanic) (California)	4317	14 162
Grand Combin (Switzerland)	4314	14 153
San Luis (Colorado)	4312	14 146
Batu (Ethiopia)	4307	14 130
Pikes Peak (Colorado)	4301	14 110
Snowmass (Colorado)	4291	14 077
Culebra (Colorado)	4286	14 070
Sunlight (Colorado)	4284	14 053
Split (California)	4283	14 051
Redcloud (Colorado)	4278	14 034
Finsteraarhorn (Switzerland)	4274	14 022
Wrangell (Alaska)	4269	14 005
Mount of the Holy Cross (Colorado)	4266	13 996
Humphreys (California)	4259	13 972

| Name | Height | |
(location)	m	ft
Ouray (Colorado)	4254	13 955
Guna (Ethiopia)	4231	13 881
Mauna Kea (Hawaii)	4205	13 796
Gannet (Wyoming)	4202	13 785
Hayes (Alaska)	4188	13 740
Fremont (Wyoming)	4185	13 730
Sidley (Antarctica)	4181	13 717
Mauna Loa (volcanic) (Hawaii)	4169	13 677
Jungfrau (Switzerland)	4158	13 642
Kings (Utah)	4124	13 528
Kinabalu (Sabah)	4102	13 455
Cameroon (volcanic) (Cameroon)	4095	13 435
Fridtjof Nansen (Antarctica)	4068	13 346
Tacaná (volcanic) (Mexico-Guatemala)	4064	13 333
Bernina (Switzerland)	4049	13 284
Summit (Colorado)	4046	13 272
Waddington (British Colombia, Canada)	4042	13 262
Lister (Antarctica)	4025	13 205

Name	Height	
(location)	m	ft
Cloud Peak (Wyoming)	4016	13 176
Yu Shan (Taiwan)	3997	13 113
Truchas (New Mexico)	3994	13 102
Wheeler (Nevada)	3981	13 058
Robson (British Colmbia, Canada)	3954	12 972
Granite (Montana)	3902	12 799
Borah (Idaho)	3858	12 655
Baldy (New Mexico)	3848	12 623
Monte Viso (Italy)	3847	12 621
Kerinci (volcanic) (Sumatra)	3805	12 483
Grossglockner (Austria)	3797	12 460
Erebus (volcanic) (Antarctica)	3794	12 447
Excelsior (California)	3790	12 434
Fujiyama (volcanic) (Japan)	3776	12 388
Cook (New Zealand)	3753	12 313
Adams (Washington)	3752	12 307
Lanín (volcanic) (Argentina-Chile)	3740	12 270
Teyde or Tenerife (volcanic) (Canary Islands)	3718	12 198

Name (location)	Height m	ft
Mahameru (volcanic) (Java)	3676	12 060
Assiniboine (British Colombia-Alberta, Canada)	3618	11 870
Hood (vocanic) (Oregon)	3428	11 245
Pico de Aneto (Spain)	3404	11 168
Rheinwaldhorn (Switzerland)	3402	11 161
Perdido (Spain)	3352	10 997
Etna (volcanic) (Sicily)	3323	10 902
Baker (Washington)	3286	10 778
Lassen (volcanic) (California)	3188	10 457
Dempo (volcanic) (Sumatra)	3159	10 364
Siple (Antarctica)	3100	10 170
Montcalm (France)	3080	10 105
Haleakala (volcanic) (Hawaii)	3058	10 032
St Helens (Washington)	2950	9677
Pulog (Philippines)	2934	9626
Tahat (Algeria)	2918	9573
Shishaldin (volcanic) (Aleutian Islands)	2862	9387
Roraima (Brazil-Venezuela-Guyana)	2810	9219

Name	Height	
(location)	m	ft
Ruapehu (volcanic)		
(New Zealand)	2797	9175
Katherine		
(Egypt)	2637	8651
Doi Inthanon		
(Thailand)	2594	8510
Galdhöpiggen		
(Norway)	2469	8100
Parnassus		
(Greece)	2457	8061
Olympus		
(Washington)	2425	7954
Kosciusko		
(Australia)	2230	7316
Harney		
(South Dakota)	2208	7242
Mitchell		
(North Carolina)	2038	6684
Clingmans Dome		
(North Carolina-Tennessee)	2025	6642
Washington		
(New Hampshire)	1917	6288
Rogers		
(Virginia)	1807	5927
Marcy		
(New York)	1629	5344
Cirque		
(Labrador)	1573	5160
Pelée (volcanic)		
(Martinique)	1463	4800

Principal Rivers of the World

Name	Length	
(location)	km	miles
Nile		
(Africa)	6695	4160
Amazon		
(South America)	6516	4050
Yangtze (Chang Jiang)		
(Asia)	6380	3965
Mississippi-Missouri		
(North America)	6019	3740
Ob'-Irtysh		
(Asia)	5570	3460
Yenisey-Angara		
(Asia)	5553	3450
Hwang Ho (Huang He)		
(Asia)	5464	3395
Zaïre		
(Africa)	4667	2900
Mekong		
(Asia)	4426	2750
Amur		
(Asia)	4416	2744
Lena		
(Asia)	4400	2730
Mackenzie		
(North America)	4250	2640
Niger		
(Africa)	4032	2505
Paraná		
(South America)	4000	2485
Missouri		
(North America)	3969	2466
Mississippi		
(North America)	3779	2348
Murray-Darling		
(Australia)	3750	2330

Name	Length	
(location)	km	miles
Volga		
(Europe)	3686	2290
Madeira		
(South America)	3203	1990
St. Lawrence		
(North America)	3203	1990
Yukon		
(North America)	3,187	1,980
Indus		
(Asia)	3180	1975
Syrdar'ya		
(Asia)	3079	1913
Salween		
(Asia)	3060	1901
Darling		
(Australia)	3057	1900
Rio Grande		
(North America)	3034	1885
São Francisco		
(South America)	2897	1800
Danube		
(Europe)	2850	1770
Brahmaputra		
(Asia)	2840	1765
Euphrates		
(Asia)	2815	1750
Pará-Tocantins		
(South America)	2752	1710
Zambezi		
(Africa)	2650	1650
Amudar'ya		
(Asia)	2620	1630
Paraguay		
(South America)	2600	1615
Nelson-Saskatchewan		
(North America)	2570	1600

Name	Length	
(location)	km	miles
Ural (Asia)	2534	1575
Kolyma (Asia)	2513	1562
Ganges (Asia)	2510	1560
Orinoco (South America)	2500	1555
Arkansas (North America)	2350	1460
Colorado (North America)	2330	1450
Xi Jiang (Asia)	2300	1427
Dnepr (Europe)	2285	1420
Negro (South America)	2254	1400
Aldan (Asia)	2242	1393
Irrawaddy (Asia)	2150	1335
Ohio (North America)	2102	1306
Orange (Africa)	2090	1299
Kama (Europe)	2028	1260
Xingú (South America)	2012	1250
Columbia (North America)	1950	1210
Juruá (South America)	1932	1200
Peace (North America)	1923	1195

Name (location)	Length km	miles
Tigris (Asia)	1900	1180
Don (Europe)	1870	1165
Pechora (Europe)	1814	1127
Araguaya (South America)	1771	1100
Snake (North America)	1670	1038
Red (North America)	1639	1018
Churchill (North America)	1610	1000
Marañón (South America)	1610	1000
Pilcomayo (South America)	1610	1000
Ucayali (South America)	1610	1000
Uruguay (South America)	1610	1000
Magdalena (South America)	1529	950
Oka (Europe)	1481	920
Canadian (North America)	1459	906
Godavari (Asia)	1449	900
Parnaíba (South America)	1449	900
Dnestr (Europe)	1411	877
Brazos (North America)	1401	870

| Name | Length | |
(location)	km	miles
Fraser		
(North America)	1368	850
Salado		
(South America)	1368	850
Rhine		
(Europe)	1320	825
Narmada		
(Asia)	1288	800
Tobol		
(Asia)	1288	800
Athabaska		
(North America)	1231	765
Pecos		
(North America)	1183	735
Green		
(North America)	1175	730
Elbe		
(Europe)	1160	720
Ottawa		
(North America)	1121	696
White		
(North America)	1111	690
Cumberland		
(North America)	1106	687
Yellowstone		
(North America)	1080	671
Donets		
(Europe)	1079	670
Tennessee		
(North America)	1050	652
Vistula		
(Europe)	1014	630
Loire		
(Europe)	1012	629
Tagus		
(Europe)	1006	625

World Facts

| Name | Length | |
(location)	km	miles
Tisza (Europe)	997	619
North Platte (North America)	995	618
Ouachita (North America)	974	605
Sava (Europe)	940	584
Neman (Europe)	937	582
Oder (Europe)	910	565
Cimarron (North America)	805	500
Gila (North America)	805	500
Gambia (Africa)	483	300

Principal Lakes of the World

| Name | Area | | Length | | Max. Depth | |
(location)	sq km	sq mi	km	mi	m	ft
Caspian (Asia-Europe)	371 000	143 205	1172	728	980	3215
Superior (North America)	83 270	32 140	564	350	393	1289
Victoria (Africa)	68 800	26 560	363	225	100	328
Aral (Asia)	65 500	25 285	379	235	68	223
Michigan (North America)	58 020	22 395	495	307	281	922

Name	Area		Length		Max. Depth	
(location)	sq km	sq mi	km	mi	m	ft
Tanganyika						
(Africa)	32 900	12 700	676	420	1435	4708
Great Bear						
(North America)	31 790	12 270	309	192	319	1047
Baykal						
(Asia)	30 500	11 775	636	395	1741	5712
Nyasa						
(Africa)	30 500	11 775	636	395	1741	5712
Great Slave						
(North America)	28 440	10 980	480	298	140	459
Erie						
(North America)	25 680	9915	388	241	64	210
Winnipeg						
(North America)	24 510	9460	429	266	21	69
Ontario						
(North America)	19 230	7425	311	193	237	778
Ladoga						
(Europe)	18 390	7100	200	124	230	755
Balkhash						
(Asia)	17 400	6715	605	376	26	85
Chad						
(Africa)	10-26 000	4-10 000	210	130	4-7	13-23
Onega						
(Europe)	9600	3705	234	145	124	407
Eyre						
(Australia)	0-8900	0-3435	145	90	0-21	0-66
Titicaca						
(South America)	8340	3220	197	122	304	997
Nicaragua						
(Central America)	8270	3190	165	102	71	230
Athabasca						
(North America)	8080	3120	335	208	92	299
Turkana						
(Africa)	7105	2743	248	154	73	240
Reindeer						
(North America)	6390	2470	250	155		

Name	Area		Length		Max. Depth	
(location)	sq km	sq mi	km	mi	m	ft
Issyk-Kul						
(Asia)	6200	2395	186	115	702	2,303
Urmia						
(Asia)	5900	2280	145	90	15	49
Torrens						
(Australia)	5780	2230	210	130		
Vänern						
(Europe)	5580	2155	147	91	98	322
Winnipegosis						
(North America)	5400	2086	227	141	12	38
Albert or Mobutu						
(Africa)	5345	2064	161	100	52	168
Mweru						
(Africa)	4921	1900	73	45	14	46
Nipigon						
(North America)	4850	1870	116	72	165	540
Manitoba						
(North America)	4700	1817	226	140		
Qinghai Hu						
(Asia)	4150	1600	110	68	39	125
Lake of the Woods						
(North America)	3850	1485	116	72	21	69
Van						
(Asia)	3710	1433	129	80	25	82
Great Salt Lake						
(North America)	2500–5000	1000–2000	121	75	11	35
Dead Sea						
(Middle East)	1020	394	74	46		

The areas of some of these lakes are subject to seasonal variations.

Principal Waterfalls of the World

Name	Height	
(location)	m	ft
Angel		
(Venezuela)	979	3212
Yosemite		
(California–including upper, central and lower falls, and rapids)		
	740	2425
Kukenaãm		
(Guyana)	610	2000
Sutherland		
(New Zealand)	581	1904
Wolloomombie		
(Australia)	519	1700
Ribbon		
(California)	492	1612
Upper Yosemite		
(California)	436	1430
Gavarnie		
(France)	422	1384
Tugela		
(South Africa)	412	1350
Takkakau		
(British Colombia)	366	1200
Staubbach		
(Switzerland)	300	984
Trümmelbach		
(Switzerland)	290	950
Middle Cascade		
(California)	278	910
Vettisfoss		
(Norway)	271	889
King Edward VIII		
(Guyana)	256	840
Gersoppa		
(India)	253	830

Name	Height	
(location)	m	ft
Skykjefos		
(Norway)	250	820
Kajeteur		
(Guyana)	226	741
Kalambo		
(Zambia)	222	726
Maradalsfos		
(Norway)	199	650
Maletsunyane		
(South Africa)	192	630
Bridalveil		
(California)	189	620
Multnomah		
(Oregon)	189	620
Vöringfoss		
(Norway)	182	597
Nevada		
(California)	181	594
Terni		
(Italy)	180	590
Skjeggedalsfoss		
(Norway)	160	525
Marina		
(Guyana)	153	500
Aughrabies		
(South Africa)	147	480
Tequendama		
(Colombia)	131	427
Guaíra		
(Brazil-Paraguay)	114	374
Illilouette		
(California)	113	370
Victoria		
(Zambia and Zimbabwe)	108	355
Kegon-no-tali		
(Japan)	101	330

Name	Height	
(location)	m	ft
Lower Yosemite (California)	98	320
Cauvery (India)	98	320
Vernal (California)	97	317
Virginia (North West Territories)	96	315
Lower Yellowstone (Wyoming)	94	308
Churchill (Labrador)	92	302
Reichenbach (Switzerland)	91	300
Sluiskin (Washington)	91	300
Lower Gastein (Austria)	86	280
Paulo Alfonso (Brazil)	84	275
Snoqualmie (Washington)	82	268
Seven (Colorado)	81	266
Montmorency (Quebec)	77	251
Handegg (Switzerland)	76	250
Taughannock (New York)	66	215
Iguassú (Brazil)	64	210
Shoshone (Idaho)	64	210
Upper Gastein (Austria)	63	207

Name	Height	
(location)	m	ft
Comet		
(Washington)	61	200
Narada		
(Washington)	52	168
Niagara		
(New York-Ontario)	51	167
Tower		
(Wyoming)	41	132
Stora Sjöfallet		
(Sweden)	40	131
Kabalega		
(Uganda)	40	130
Upper Yellowstone		
(Wyoming)	34	109